Praise for Loyalty 3.0

"Relationships are the single greatest asset for all organizations. Relationships with customers, relationships with employees, relationships with partners. In Loyalty 3.0, Rajat Paharia reveals the new science of relationship building through big data and gamification."
— Tim Brown, CEO, IDEO

"The journey to Loyalty 3.0 is real. Rajat's vision shows why right time relevancy and context will transform how organizations engage with customers and truly craft relationships."
— R. Ray Wang, Principal Analyst and CEO at Constellation Research

"Adoption is a critical component when creating an exceptional customer experience or smarter workforce, and gamification has proven to be a powerful driver for success. The insights Rajat shares in Loyalty 3.0 will help guide the next wave of deeper relationships across the enterprise."
— Sandy Carter, IBM Vice President, Social Business Evangelism and Sales

"Loyalty 3.0 is filled with major insights and does a brilliant job of grounding the reader in fundamental concepts around motivation, big data, and gamification—building on these concepts through real-world case studies that bring the combinations to life. It finishes with actionable ideas and next steps that enable you to test and operationalize these ideas in your own workplace and personal life."
— Brad Smith, CEO, Intuit

A *fascinating insight into how companies are exploiting big data."*
—Mark Read, CEO, WPP Digital

"*Rajat pioneered the business use of big data and game mechanics to transform the customer experience. A decade before anyone else, he saw that the same techniques that video game designers had used for years—fast feedback, badges, competition, goals, and leveling up—were also incredibly powerful for motivating behavior outside of games, and an industry was born. This book shares his secrets.*"
—Clara Shih, CEO of Hearsay Social,
author of *The Facebook Era,*
and board member at Starbucks

"*Rajat Paharia comprehensively explains how to create loyalty in the modern world full of data and connectivity. If you want to learn how to motivate and inspire employees, you must read this book.*"
—Dave Kerpen, New York Times bestselling author
of *Likeable Social Media* and *Likeable Business*

"*In this powerful and groundbreaking book, Rajat Paharia clearly demonstrates how big data, motivation, and gamification can be utilized to create true engagement and loyalty. We believe Loyalty 3.0 will be a game changer for our associates and guests.*"
—Ray Bennett, Chief Lodging Services Officer,
Marriott International

LOYALTY
3.0

LOYALTY
3.0

How **BIG DATA** and **GAMIFICATION**
Are Revolutionizing Customer
and Employee Engagement

RAJAT PAHARIA

New York Chicago San Francisco Lisbon London Madrid Mexico City
Milan New Delhi San Juan Sydney Toronto

1 2 3 4 5 6 7 8 9 0   DOC/DOC   1 8 7 6 5 4 3

ISBN: 978-0-07-181337-2
MHID: 0-07-181337-3

e-ISBN: 978-0-07-181338-9
e-MHID: 0-07-181338-1

Library of Congress Cataloging-in-Publication Data
Paharia, Rajat.
  Loyalty 3.0 : how to revolutionize customer and employee engagement with big data and gamification / by Rajat Paharia.
      pages cm
  ISBN-13: 978-0-07-181337-2 (alk. paper)
  ISBN-10: 0-07-181337-3 (alk. paper)
  1. Brand loyalty. 2. Customer relations. 3. Marketing–Management. 4. Corporate culture. 5. Organizational behavior. I. Title.
  HF5415.32.P34 2013
  658.8'12–dc23
                              2013004837

McGraw-Hill books are available at special quantity discounts to use as premiums and sales promotions, or for use in corporate training programs. To contact a representative, please visit the Contact Us page at www.mhprofessional.com.

This book is printed on acid-free paper.

Disclosures

The following companies named in this book are (or have been) either a customer or a partner of Bunchball, directly or indirectly:

Adobe

Bluewolf

BOX

Chiquita Brands

Comcast

CrowdFlower

Eloqua

Ford of Canada

HP

HopeLab

IBM

Intuit

Jive Software

Kraft Canada

LiveOps

Maritz Canada

Microsoft

MTV

NBCUniversal

Oracle

Redding.com

Right Guard

Salesforce.com

SAP

SolarWinds

Tableau

Universal Studios

USA Network

Warner Bros.

Wendy's

For More Information

Visit the Loyalty 3.0 website at www.loyalty30.com.

To Riley, Jake, Evan, and Laura

Contents

Acknowledgments

First and foremost, I'd like to thank Bunchball's customers, employees, partners, advisers, and investors. Without you and your support, none of this would have been possible.

Our customers have always been forward-thinkers who understand that engagement, motivation, and loyalty are key competitive advantages in their industries. I'm honored that we've been able to earn their business, and every day we get out of bed thinking about how to serve them better. I'd like to thank them all, particularly the ones that contributed to the case studies in this book.

I love going to work every day because I work with amazing people doing work that we're proud of, making our customers happy, and solving challenging problems together. To everyone who has worked at Bunchball in the past, is there now, and will join us in the future—you have my undying gratitude. I know that you get to vote with your feet, and I'm grateful that you've chosen to direct your feet here and contribute to our vision. I'd like to explicitly thank my current crop of MVPs (and BFFs), including Christian Battaglia, Alexis Bley, Alyssa Bentley, Michael Bosworth, Gary Chavez, Kyle Clark, Joseph Cole, Keith Conley, Jim Cumella, Caitlin Donaldson, Danny Drobnitch, Sharif Elgamal, Angelina Elhassan, John Evangelista, Joe Fisher, Matt Foster, Kevin Freitas, Sudhanshu Gaur, Mitch Gilbert, Katherine Heisler, Mark Herstek, Tina Hou, Deepti Illa, Caroline Japic, Jackie Jones, Ken Jones, Dan Katz, Barry Kirk, Andrew Kirpalani, Molly Kittle, Mary Lahlouh, Vivian Lin, Lucy Lopez, Kasey McCurdy, Rob Mullany, Jim Normandin, Purvi Patel, Stacy Rademacher, Robert Richards, Ramiro Rodriguez, Jim Scullion, Anupam Singhal, Scott Sorge, Kevin

Spier, Chris Sullivan, Ed Van Petten, Aparna Vasireddi, Yiran Wang, Matthew Williams, and Arjan van Ham.

In particular, I'd like to give special shout-outs to Anupam Singhal, Molly Kittle, and Kevin Spier for their years of passion and dedication; Caroline Japic for making this book happen; and Jim Scullion for his mentorship and leadership.

I started Bunchball with Sunil Singh, who worked with me to refine our ideas and turn them into actual product, and who served as a valued sounding board for years. And our first outside angel investor was Payman Pouladdej, who out-of-the-blue handed me a check at a Starbucks and left me speechless for the first time in a very long time. Thank you both for your belief, guidance, and friendship.

Back in 2005 and 2006, I was pitching our ideas to any venture capitalist who would listen, and everyone said "No." I'd like to thank Chris Hollenbeck at Granite Ventures and John Leckrone at Adobe Ventures for saying "Yes" and betting on an unproven entrepreneur with ideas that were not obvious and certainly not what everyone else was doing. In particular, Chris has had the patience and foresight to support the company through the inevitable ups and downs and the start up curse of being too early to a market. Since then, we've added a great group of investors to our family, including Mike Morgan and Dain DeGroff from Triangle Peak Partners, Tyson Morgan from Northport Investments, and Trevor Kienzle from Correlation Ventures. Many thanks to all of you for your continued support.

We're fortunate to have an incredibly strong bench of talent and experience on our board of directors and advisory board, and I'd like to thank them all for lending their vision and expertise to us, including Ken Klein, Doug Dennerline, Jason Blessing, Jeff Diana, and Kelly Kay.

From McGraw-Hill, I'd like to thank Donya Dickerson for shepherding this book from inception to publication and Leila Porteous for planting the initial seed in my brain that I should write a book on this important topic.

I'd like to thank my family for their support over the years. My parents, Ram and Kusum Paharia, both immigrants from India and engineers in Silicon Valley, encouraged education, instilled a strong work ethic, and supported my love of technology from an early age. And my sister, Neeru Paharia, who surpassed us all in education with a Ph.D. in behavioral economics from the Harvard Business School and is now a professor at Georgetown University. I'd also like to thank my in-laws, Larry and Peggy Pfeifer; Mark, Caryn, Julia, and Andy Pfeifer; Nick, Kristin, Will, and Avery Pfeifer; and Jen and House Domonkos just for being awesome.

My sons, Riley, Jake, and Evan Paharia, have added three new dimensions to my life, and I can't imagine it any other way. Thank you for all your love, unbridled energy, and lust for life. Daddy also would appreciate it if you'd let him sleep in once in a while.

Finally, everything falls apart without my wife, Laura Paharia, at my side. Thank you for keeping me sane, being my sounding board, loving and taking care of our family, eliminating excess commas in my writing, introducing me to the wonders of semicolons, and being my partner in life. You're brilliant, compassionate, and dedicated, and even though I'll never win at a board or card game again, I consider myself incredibly lucky.

Introduction

Six years ago, back in May 2007, I had a decision to make. Bunchball, the company I had started and was the CEO of, could follow one of two paths. Either path could make or break the company, but a choice had to be made because we were a small team of 14 and couldn't follow both. How was I supposed to decide?

A little background is probably in order. I started Bunchball in 2005, inspired by my in-laws at Thanksgiving. Every year, 30+ family members from around the country would converge on a small four-bedroom, one-and-a-half-bathroom house in suburban Detroit and spend several days playing. This was a family that loved games—board games, card games, video games—it didn't matter, as long as they were playing (and drinking!) together. Then, after Thanksgiving, everyone would go to their respective homes, and there was no fun to be had together for the rest of the year, until the next Thanksgiving rolled around.

I sensed an opportunity, a way to use technology to enable our distributed family members to continue to play casual games together even when geographically dispersed. I could build a platform that enabled users to create groups with their family members and then play either real-time games together if everyone was online at the same time or turn-based games that could be played whenever someone had a free minute.

In 2005, this was a revelation. At the time, it was really easy to play games online by yourself or with random strangers, but playing with your friends and family online was really hard, if not impossible. In the real world, though, that was how we spent almost all our playtime—with people we already knew. Something had been lost in the migration of games to the online world, and there was an opportunity to fill the gap.

Inspired by this vision of enabling people to "Play with your friends" online, I launched Bunchball. The company name came to me in the shower, as the best ideas often do. I had been trying to think of a name that conveyed the concept that you no longer went to a game first and then picked or were matched with whomever was there but that you'd bring your friends and family with you and move from game to game to game.

When kids play soccer, they often move around in a mob—someone kicks the ball, and the mob (or bunch) follows because they want to be where the action is. Positions? Yeah, right. Parents and coaches call this *bunchball*, and the name captured what we were trying to accomplish perfectly.

We started Bunchball as a destination site at bunchball. com, where users would come, set up their groups, and play games. The site made its public debut in October 2005. As we learned and received feedback from our users, the vision evolved from being a destination site, to being distributed gaming widgets on social networks such as MySpace, to being a multiplayer casual gaming service that was sold to online publishers and community owners to enhance the community on their sites. We called it *social gaming*.

In the process of building this social-gaming platform, we uncovered two things. First were the techniques that video game designers had used for years to motivate their players to be more engaged and loyal—things such as fast feedback, badges, competition, goals, leveling up, and community. We were astounded at the power these techniques had to motivate the players in our games. Second was that these techniques could be used outside the gaming world to motivate any kind of behavior, among any kind of audience, because they tapped into fundamental human motivators. While digging for gold in social games, we had chanced upon a diamond, one with the ability to focus user activity and attention while at the same time engaging and motivating people.

Innovation = invention + opportunity, and in early 2007, we saw an opportunity to innovate in the field of engagement and loyalty by taking these techniques that had been invented in the gaming world and applying them outside games, and by building a technology platform that any online business could use to motivate its customers. We refocused the company on building this *motivation engine* in earnest and started winding down our social-games business.

Which brings us back to May 2007 and my dilemma. Facebook had unexpectedly launched its application platform and had invited us to be one of it's launch partners with our social-gaming product. Figuring we had nothing to lose, we accepted, and so we were the first gaming company on Facebook. Overnight, use of our social-gaming platform exploded, and our servers were catching fire.

Once we had contained the fires, we had a decision to make. Our initial vision that social games were a killer app for social networks was now, years later, coming to fruition. We had seen the future, but we had just been too early. Should we now go back to the business we had just convinced our employees and investors to abandon, social games, and bet on growing a big user base on Facebook and then figuring out how to make money from it (which nobody had at that point)? Or should we continue to wind down the social games and execute our new vision, a complete unknown but with the opportunity to change the world by bringing technology to bear on the problem of human motivation, engagement, and loyalty? With limited time, money, and people, we had to pick one.

In the end, the opportunity to change the world won. We abandoned the social-gaming business and focused completely on this new field, which would come to be known as *gamification*. We started in the world of media, publishing, and communities, working with customers such as NBCUniversal and Comcast to drive engagement and loyalty among their fans and members. Much as we had been from 2005–2006 in the social gaming space, we were ahead of our time, and it took several years for the market to catch up with us. Once again, we had seen the future, but this time we were determined to stay the course—the opportunity was too big to let go.

In 2010 the market finally did catch up, with the success of companies such as Foursquare and social games such as Farmville that exposed hundreds of millions of people to the power of gamification. More and more companies started using gamification to engage their customers, and then in 2011 they started using it to engage and motivate their employees and partners as well. And along with this explosion in the use of gamification by businesses, there's been a corresponding increase in conferences, books, companies, consultants providing gamification services, and analysts commenting about the space.

In the intervening years, we have continued to expand and refine our vision, with the latest research on motivation, loyalty, behavioral economics, and design, as well as the latest trends and technologies. We've also worked with hundreds of companies across a range of industries around the world. And we see, clearly, the macro trends that are reshaping the world of customer, partner, and employee engagement. Chief among these is the fact that we're now living our lives online—community, entertainment, work, finances—everything we do is being mediated by technology and, as a result, is throwing off reams of data (*big data*) about our activity. Smart companies, forward-thinking companies, are feeding this user-activity data into gamification systems, which use data-driven motivational techniques (the very same ones that we "discovered" in 2007) to drive engagement, high-value activity, and loyalty.

I wrote this book to share what we've learned with you and arm you with everything you need to know to build a loyalty and engagement program that drives a competitive advantage for your business. Part 1, "Vision," is the foundation; it lays out the core vision of *Loyalty 3.0* and the three building blocks that make it possible: motivation, big data, and gamification. Part 2, "Execution," provides a number of case studies that describe how innovative companies are already using these principles to drive customer engagement, learning and skill development, and employee motivation, while realizing meaningful business results. Finally, Part 3, "Direction," gives you the road map—the step-by-step guide on how to plan, design, build, and optimize your program.

When searching for the right word to describe this new field, the word that kept surfacing, over and over, in the shower and out of the shower, was *loyalty*. The only problem was that the word, as used by the loyalty industry for the last hundred years, had come to mean something completely different. So we decided that it was time to take back the word *loyalty* and to evolve it to meet the needs of today's businesses.

Welcome to *Loyalty 3.0*.

VISION

The first step towards getting somewhere
is to decide that you are not going
to stay where you are.

J.P. Morgan

CHAPTER 1

May You Live in Interesting Times

The Three Faces of Loyalty

When you think of the word *loyalty* in the context of business, what comes to mind? If you're like most people, the first thing that will pop into your head is a typical loyalty program, where you earn points for your purchases and can redeem them for rewards. These programs are meant to drive *customer* loyalty, and according to studies,[1] you're probably a member of 18 of them. And yet I'm willing to bet that you're deeply ambivalent about all of them and, if given a better offer by another business, would gladly defect. These programs, on which billions of dollars are spent annually, aren't generating loyalty to a business; they're generating loyalty to the best deal and so are completely failing at their fundamental purpose.

What is that purpose? It's to give customers a compelling reason to continue to patronize the business and to resist competitive offers. If a new store opens across the street or a competitor slashes prices, businesses with loyal customers won't lose those customers because they've elevated their relationship from a transactional one to something more meaningful. They have engaged those customers.

Now let's switch gears to *employees*, arguably a company's biggest asset. Shouldn't the same thinking apply to them? Managers want their employees to be loyal so that employees perform to the best of their abilities, do what's best for the company, and resist competitive employment offers. Yet, while businesses acknowledge that they want loyal employees, most are not actually doing anything about it. They spend billions attempting to engage their customers and a fraction of that, if anything, on engaging their employees.

Finally, companies today rarely accomplish anything alone. You work with *partners* to source critical raw materials, enhance product offerings, and amplify your sales efforts. The efforts of these partners are critical to the success of your business, so you need those partners to be engaged. You need them to be loyal. And yet again, we find that today's businesses generally have only rudimentary, if any, systems in place to drive that loyalty. And what systems they do have in place feel remarkably like the 18 loyalty programs that consumers are ambivalent about.

Clearly, something needs to change. And the companies that figure it out, that create true loyalty, are going to realize a sizable and sustainable competitive advantage and win in their markets.

The Road to *Loyalty 3.0*

Loyalty 3.0 is about taking back the word *loyalty* and making it actually mean something. It does this by combining the latest research on human motivation with the big data generated by your customers, partners, and employees as they interact with you to empower your business to motivate, engage, and create true loyalty.

But before we can understand where we're going, we need to understand where we've been.

Loyalty 1.0

We all know Loyalty 1.0 programs; they're the frequent-flyer programs, cash-back credit cards, and "buy ten get one free" punch cards from the local sandwich shop that have been around for many years. These are purely transactional, completely focused on customers, and absolute failures at generating the kind of loyalty that businesses actually want. For customers, at best, they're mildly pleasing, and at worst, when a business isn't living up to its brand promise, they feel like a way for a business to hold them hostage. For businesses, at best, they're table stakes in an industry where everyone else has one, and at worst, they're a giant cost center eating into the bottom line and creating a huge liability.

Loyalty 1.0 programs also suffer from fundamental structural problems. There's an exciting part at the beginning when you sign up for the program and dream about how you're going to earn spectacular rewards and another at the end (if you get there) when you actually redeem for a (possibly spectacular but maybe not) reward. In the middle is just a very long grind with no motivation, no engagement, and no loyalty being generated. There's a gulf of lost opportunity in the middle.

Loyalty 2.0

In the early 1990s, 1-to-1 marketing emerged, focused primarily on making the loyalty experience more targeted through segmentation and personalization, with a big emphasis on direct-mail and e-mail campaigns. Data had a bigger role here as businesses took the information they were learning about their customers and used it to "speak to their interests." While this was effective for a while, open rates on these communications plummeted as the overall level of direct mail and e-mail increased. Consumers were overwhelmed by the sheer amount of noise, and the problem has only gotten worse.

Loyalty 3.0

After Loyalty 2.0, things got stuck for a while. Sure, new technology meant that you could now interact with your loyalty program from your mobile phone and that you could build a Facebook page for your brand, but nothing fundamentally changed. Not until now, when the pieces have finally come together to enable Loyalty 3.0. Loyalty 3.0 has three major enabling components that, when combined, are much greater than the sum of the parts:

1. **Motivation.** Recent social-science research has much more clearly defined what compels and motivates human behavior, and what causes people to do things or not do things in life and in the workplace. Knowing what truly motivates people—and what doesn't—enables us to create stronger engagement and true loyalty.

2. **Big data.** Technology has taken over how we communicate, socialize, work, and play. The amount of data that people are generating as they interact with these systems is exploding, and new technology is enabling businesses to capture that data with more granularity than ever before. Smart businesses can consume this data and use it to understand, engage, and motivate their constituents in ways not previously possible.

3. **Gamification.** Game designers have been using data-driven motivational techniques for years. Our new understanding of motivation, combined with the emergence of big

data streams, has enabled these techniques to be used outside the gaming world, where they can be powerful tools to drive engagement, participation, and high-value activity for customers, employees, and partners alike. (See Figure 1.1)

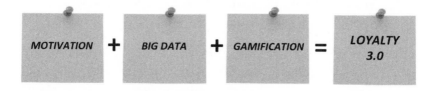

Figure 1.1 THE LOYALTY 3.0 EQUATION.

By leveraging these three components together, we can make our customers, partners, and employees more engaged, more active, and truly loyal. We'll spend the next few chapters in Part 1 covering the building blocks on the left side of the equation—motivation, big data, and gamification. In Part 2 we'll take a deep dive into numerous case studies of companies that have successfully used Loyalty 3.0 in their businesses so that you can see exactly how it works in the real world. And we'll finish up in Part 3 with a step-by-step guide that will walk you through the creation of your own Loyalty 3.0 program.

The Four Tiers of Loyalty

Barry Kirk, my colleague at Bunchball and a veteran of the loyalty industry, wrote eloquently in *Chief Marketer*[2] about the various tiers of loyalty that people *really* experience. See if any of these sound familiar to you:

- **Inertia loyalty.** If a brand's loyalty strategy involves such terms as *barrier to exit*, it most likely falls into the inertia loyalty category—making it inconvenient to leave the program rather than irresistible to stay. Customers in this tier stick around because it's too inconvenient to escape. Classic examples include airline loyalty programs (where a lack of alternate flights produces loyalty) or banks and grocery stores (where loyalty is often proximity-based). With inertia loyalty, customers have no incentive to stay once a competitor makes it easy to switch.

- **Mercenary loyalty.** Just as a mercenary will swear allegiance for a price, marketers can pay or "bribe" customers for their loyalty. Most traditional points- and discounts-based loyalty programs operate in this tier because of past effectiveness, but the industry now sees a leveling off of participation rates for this type of program. Yes, the tactic may work, but its major weakness is that the loyalty generated is emotionally shallow—it's simply about getting freebies or a better price; these programs amount to a complex method of discounting. Here, too, there's little to stop your competitor from taking customers simply by discounting or paying more.

- **True loyalty.** Brands reach this tier when a customer has a compelling reason—ideally, an emotional stake in the brand—to resist competitive offers. If a new store opens across the street or a competitor slashes prices, a brand with true loyalty won't lose customers because the relationship is based on a deeper connection of trust and shared value. Good examples include Starbucks (people go out of their way to spend more for it) or Chipotle (which appeals to consumers' values around sustainability and humanely treated animals). All brands can attain true loyalty if they are committed to a win-win relationship with their customers.

- **Cult loyalty.** Ever see someone who proudly sports a brand logo as her favorite tattoo? Or maybe just a friend who consistently refers to himself as a "____ guy" (fill in his favorite brand name). At the cult loyalty tier, the customer and the brand begin to merge so that rejecting the brand would be like rejecting your own values. Customer commitment becomes a virtual lock at that level (congrats to Harley-Davidson, Apple, and Coca-Cola). Unfortunately for marketers, cult loyalty is next to impossible to artificially manufacture. It emerges only organically—but once it does, it can be cultivated.

The goal of Loyalty 3.0 and this book is to show you the way to true loyalty, not just for your customers but for your employees and partners as well.

What Is Engagement?

There seem to be as many definitions of *engagement* as there are people. My favorite is from Forrester Research,[3] where engagement is defined as having three parts:

- A deep emotional connection with the brand
- High levels of active participation
- A long-term relationship

Note the point about active participation—engaged constituents don't just feel, they act. They participate, advocate, ideate, contribute, and generally engage in high-value activity that makes your business better. What this definition makes clear is that the path to true loyalty is through engagement.

We Live in Interesting Times

While on the surface this sounds like a blessing (who wouldn't want to live in interesting times?), it is in fact meant to be a curse. In a speech in Capetown, South Africa, in 1966, Robert Kennedy explained:

> *There is a Chinese curse which says, "May he live in interesting times." Like it or not, we live in interesting times. They are times of danger and uncertainty, but they are also more open to the creative energy of men than any other time in history.*[4]

Fast forward to today, and the world of business is experiencing its own "danger and uncertainty." The rate of business change is faster than ever before, technology is disrupting everything, and companies are rising and falling at warp speed. If you're looking at this maelstrom with the right lens, however, you can see that a series of important trends is converging and making engagement and true loyalty essential to the success of any business. For those who can see the signs and steer their businesses in the right direction, opportunity awaits.

We're Living in the Age of Distraction

We are living in a crowded, 24/7, global marketplace — a "flat world." Your customers are confronted with more competing messages, more options, and more distractions than ever before — more websites, more social media platforms, more media vehicles, and more mobile applications, all aggressively fighting for their attention. Over a billion people now spend hours each day sharing, posting, tweeting, and commenting on social networks. And they're doing it everywhere — at home, at work, at school, waiting for the train, and at the dinner table. They are always "on."

Amid this never-ending cacophony, how do you earn and maintain customer attention? Because customers will buy from the businesses that most effectively engage with them, whereas disengaged customers will grow disinterested, delay purchases, abandon carts, and wander off to competitors. Businesses need to cut through the clutter and engage their customers to prevent their messages and relationships from being lost in the noise.

The Workforce Has Disengaged

According to Gallup surveys,[5] 70 percent of people who go to work every day aren't engaged in their jobs, costing the U.S. economy up to $350 billion per year in lost productivity. These disengaged employees are unproductive and are just as likely as disengaged customers to defect. And disengagement can be viral, spreading from one department to the next, leaving entire teams frustrated and unmotivated.

Engaged workers, on the other hand, can drive meaningful increases in productivity, profitability, and product quality, as well as less absenteeism, turnover, and shrinkage. Given the benefits, it's imperative that businesses figure out how to engage their employees in a scalable, cost-effective manner.

Social Media Have Changed the Power Dynamic

Social media have fundamentally changed how we interact with each other and with businesses. Sites such as Facebook and Twitter have ushered in a new era in which businesses no longer control the conversation. In the *broadcast* era, businesses controlled the means of transmission at scale, and all consumers could do was to passively receive. In the social era, the rules have changed. Peer-to-peer conversations about a company and its products have become as important as the company's communications, if not more so. Recent Nielsen studies[6] tell us that 92 percent of consumers trust a peer recommendation compared to a 29 to 47 percent trust rate for company advertisements.

Consumers now can have their own discussions about businesses and brands, with or without the brand's involvement, and can voice their opinions on a global scale for everyone to hear. Opinion, kudos, and dissatisfaction all can spread globally, like wildfire, completely outside a company's control. As a result, companies need to engage their customers and work to make them advocates, not instigators.

Corporate Information Technology Is Being Consumerized

The consumerization of computing and personal technology has been going on for years—what started in the military made its way into business and then into the home. Cheap, easy-to-access, easy-to-use PCs, tablets, and smart phones have spread to most corners of the earth.

What's new today is the consumerization of the corporate information technology (IT) landscape. For decades, we all used more technology at work than at home, and because of that, our expectations of technology were set by our experiences at work. Technology vendors designed primarily for the work context, and our employers dictated the technology that we used in a top-down, command-and-control manner.

The balance has shifted in recent years, and now we're all using as much, if not more, technology at home as at work. And we're bringing that home-based technology into the workplace, where it's working its way into our companies bottom up. What starts with an individual using BOX for cloud storage or an iPad for mobile work quickly turns into teams, entire business units, and entire companies using these technologies.

And what happens when those consumer technologies, with their user experiences designed for ease of use, simplicity, and delight, are contrasted with the existing enterprise platforms for collaboration, expense reporting, and human resources? The enterprise systems pale in comparison, and workers demand better. *Functional* isn't good enough anymore; business technology now needs to be usable, simple, and engaging.

Generation Y Is on the Ascent

The emergence of Generation Y (also called *Millenials*), people born from the early eighties to the mid-nineties, as a demographic force is driving dramatic change in education, technology, media, and most critically, at work. There are currently 80 million Millenials in the United States, and every day another 10,000 of them turn 21.[7] They make up 25 percent of the workforce today,[8] and by 2025, that number is expected to increase to 75 percent—three of every four workers globally will be from Generation Y.[9]

Millennials are "digital natives." They live and breathe online—play, school, and now work. They're accustomed to cutting-edge technology and innovation at home and expect the same quality of technology in the workplace. They've grown up with and expect always-on instant communication coupled with real-time feedback and responses to their creations and communications. They've also grown up in a time of rapid change, where *new* becomes *normal* overnight, so engaging them requires evolving, changing, and constantly staying fresh.

They have been playing video games—console, mobile, social, massively multiplayer online role-playing games (MMORPGs), and more—since childhood and thus have been immersed in the language and metaphors of gaming their entire lives. In studies conducted by MTV in 2011 and 2012, Millennials reported that a "game-like metaphor" applied to almost every aspect of their life. More than half also reported that "people my age see real life as a video game" and "winning is the slogan of my generation."[10] They also think they're better players in the "game of work," with more than

75 percent thinking that they'd know how to "level up" faster than others.[11]

Given their demographic impact, it's imperative that businesses figure out how to engage and motivate Generation Y at scale by addressing their unique characteristics and desires and interacting with them in a way that resonates with their views on life.

Workforces Are Distributed

The changing nature of work, coupled with enabling technology, has created a boom in distributed workforces. Businesses worldwide are fast realizing the benefits associated with allowing employees to work from home: reduced real estate costs, the ability to recruit and retain quality employees who want flexibility, more time spent actually working instead of commuting, and the opportunity to provide superior local service. IBM, for instance, estimates that 40 percent of its 400,000 global employees are working remotely—either from home or on-site at a client. And according to a 2011 study by Telework Research Network,[12] 45 percent of the U.S. workforce holds a job that is suitable for part- or full-time telecommuting.

This doesn't come without its challenges, however. Remote workers suffer from management mistrust ("How do I know they're working?"), poor visibility into their colleagues' activity, having to discipline themselves to work when the lines between work and life are blurry, jobs that often don't have clear and measurable success metrics, and a reduction in opportunities to engage with their colleagues—both formally and informally. Businesses that are able to address these issues and use technology to bring their distributed workforce closer together, even when their members are physically apart, will benefit from the best of both worlds.

There's Too Much to Learn

The software that we use, the cars that we drive, the taxes that we file, and the microwave ovens that we try to program—none of it is getting easier. Technology has brought us amazing innovation and, along with it, amazing complexity. So how do you expect your customers to learn about all your offerings, your employees to learn all the tools of their trade, and your partners to learn how to sell all your products? In a world where people will spend four hours playing Angry Birds but won't spend five minutes going through training to learn something new, businesses that can engage their constituents and motivate them to learn and develop new skills will have a huge advantage in the marketplace.

Software Is Eating the World

Marc Andreessen, serial entrepreneur turned venture capitalist, coined this phrase[13] to describe how software is "eating" traditional businesses—enabled by global broadband and mobile Internet penetration (a big market), free software programming tools (a low barrier to entry), and infrastructure available on-demand (the ability to scale quickly and cheaply). Examples of software eating the world include Skype disrupting the communication market, Netflix dominating movie rentals, and digital music companies such as Spotify, Pandora, and Apple's iTunes dominating the music industry.

The side benefit to all this "eating" is that as we engage with these systems, they are generating streams of big data about how we're interacting with them, data that smart companies can and will use to motivate us and drive our engagement and loyalty. We'll learn about that shortly, but first we need to understand human motivation.

Building Loyalty 3.0

Loyalty 3.0 expands upon traditional loyalty in various ways.

- Traditional loyalty has failed to drive loyalty to anything but a deal.

- Loyalty 3.0 is about engagement, a deeper connection with the participant.

- Loyalty 3.0 has three parts—motivation, big data, and gamification—and engages three constituents—customers, partners, and employees.

- Macro trends are making Loyalty 3.0 an essential business requirement.
  - We're living in the age of distraction.
  - The workforce has disengaged.
  - Social media have changed the power dynamic.
  - Corporate IT is being consumerized.
  - Generation Y is on the ascent.
  - Workforces are distributed.
  - There's too much to learn.
  - Software is eating the world.

CHAPTER 2

Whoever Figures Out Motivation Wins

Fueling the Fire

L oyalty 3.0 has two primary sources of fuel—one is big data, which we'll discuss in Chapter 3, and the other is human motivation. Here's the amazing thing about human motivation: If you can tap into it properly, there's a never-ending supply of it. It's like cold fusion for loyalty. And whoever figures out how to harness that energy is going to win.

We should start by defining *motivation*. Since we're talking about it in the context of business, let's use the definition from BusinessDictionary.com:

> *Internal and external factors that stimulate desire and energy in people to be continually interested in and committed to a job, role, or subject, and to exert persistent effort in attaining a goal.*

> *Motivation results from the interactions among conscious and unconscious factors such as the:*

> 1. *intensity of desire or need*
> 2. *incentive or reward value of the goal*

3. *expectations of the individual and of his or her significant others.*[1]

Let's break the first part of the definition down and understand its parts:

- **Internal and external factors.** Motivation can come from within a person as well as from outside a person. We'll discuss the difference between intrinsic (internal) motivators and extrinsic (external) motivators below.
- **That stimulate desire and energy in people.** This is the cold-fusion part of motivation, our inexhaustible "desire and energy."
- **To be continually interested in and committed to a job, role, or subject.** Our "desire and energy" have a context.
- **And to exert persistent effort.** Remember, Loyalty 3.0 isn't about passively receiving; it's about action.
- **In attaining a goal.** At the end of the day, the person is motivated to accomplish or achieve something. It has some "reward value."

Based on research from leading academics who have studied motivation (who we'll discuss in greater detail momentarily), combined with our years of experience in real-world applications, we believe that there are five key intrinsic motivators for Loyalty 3.0:

- **Autonomy** is the urge to direct our own lives (*"I control"*).
- **Mastery** is the desire to get better at something that matters (*"I improve"*).
- **Purpose** is the yearning to do what we do in the service of something larger than ourselves (*"I make a difference"*).

- **Progress** is the desire to see results in the direction of mastery and the greater purpose (*"I achieve"*).

- **Social interaction** is the need to belong and to be connected to and interact with others (*"I connect with others"*).

These motivations are innate, not learned, and have been proven to be universal, across cultures, age groups, and time.

Note that we explicitly called these out as *intrinsic* motivators. As we saw from our definition earlier, motivation is either intrinsic (initiating an activity for its own sake because it is interesting and satisfying in itself) or extrinsic (some external force is influencing, motivating, or requiring you to do something). Most theories of motivation state that intrinsic motivators are more powerful than extrinsic motivators. Often people will read these theories and come to the conclusion that intrinsic equals good and extrinsic equals bad. There are a lot of reasons for this, because of studies that have been done over the years that demonstrate the failures of extrinsic motivators in certain scenarios and also, I believe, because people inherently want to believe that something innate and intrinsic must be better because it comes from within.

There are no doubt problems with extrinsic motivators—studies have shown that extrinsic motivators can "extinguish" intrinsic motivation. If a child loves to play the piano and then you enter her into piano competitions and push her to win, Win, WIN, the natural joy she derived from playing disappears, and playing becomes something she has to do rather than something she wants to do. The extrinsic motivator of competition has extinguished her natural joy and love of making music.

In his book, *The Upside of Irrationality: The Unexpected Benefits of Defying Logic at Work and at Home*, Duke University professor and author Dan Ariely describes studies that show that extrinsic motivators can lead to a decrease in performance for creative work. And author Alfie Kohn has written an entire book on the topic called, *Punished by Rewards—The Trouble with Gold Stars, Incentive Plans, A's, Praise, and Other Bribes*, in which he cites studies demonstrating that people do inferior work when enticed with money, grades, and other incentives.

It's all true, but it doesn't mean that extrinsic motivators are bad, just that they should be used carefully, in the appropriate contexts, and in a way that doesn't extinguish any existing intrinsic motivation. In his book, *Drive: The Surprising Truth About What Motivates Us*, author Daniel Pink describes tasks as being one of two types:

- **Algorithmic.** You follow a set of rules or a checklist to complete a task. Examples might include doing taxes, checking out at the grocery store, and assembling cars. Since these tasks are rule-based, they also lend themselves to automation.

- **Heuristic.** There is no algorithm, no set of rules, and no checklist. You have to be creative and figure out the solution. Writing a book, designing a new product, and crafting a marketing strategy are all examples of heuristic tasks. These kinds of tasks are much harder to automate than algorithmic tasks.[2]

Algorithmic tasks typically don't engender much intrinsic motivation, and in those cases, extrinsic motivators can work very well. Heuristic tasks, on the other hand, depend on intrinsic creativity and motivation to be successful. So a heavy-handed use of extrinsic motivators, as in the example of the young girl playing the piano, can have the opposite of the desired effect. According to Pink, because algorithmic work is so easily automated and outsourced, it accounts for only 30 percent of the job growth in the United States, whereas the remaining 70 percent comes from heuristic work. The future, it would seem, is heuristic.

And people are complex—it's not always easy to figure out what is motivating them to do something. As opposed to treating them as binary opposites, another way to view intrinsic and extrinsic motivation is as two ends of a spectrum—motivation sometimes falls cleanly into either category but often lies somewhere in between. Take something as simple as going to the gym and working out. Did you do it for the sheer innate joy of running hard on a treadmill or feeling that good soreness in your arm muscles after a hard workout? Did you do it because you want to be fit? Because you want to lose weight? Because you want to be stronger? Why do you want those things? So that you feel better about yourself? So that other people notice you more, compliment you, or want to go out with you? So here's the question: Are you intrinsically motivated to go to the gym or extrinsically motivated? The answer, I think, is both.

Much of the research on motivation that we're going to reference here is taken from studies done in the workplace, but it applies just as well to our personal lives. Our fundamental nature doesn't change as soon as we walk in or out of the workplace door, and the same things that work to motivate us at work will work at home, and vice versa.

Deep Dive into the Five Intrinsic Motivators

Now that we understand the difference between intrinsic and extrinsic motivators, it's time for a closer look at the five key intrinsic motivators for Loyalty 3.0. Three of the five motivators form the foundation of *self-determination theory* (SDT),[3] a theory of motivation created by a pair of University of Rochester professors, Drs. Edward L. Deci and Richard M. Ryan. To these motivators we have added two additional ones that other academics have identified and that our experience has shown to have strong motivational effects. We will take a closer look at extrinsic motivators in Chapter 4 when we discuss gamification.

Autonomy—"I Control"

Autonomy, as noted earlier, is the "urge to direct our own lives" and is the first pillar of SDT. We want to be in control; we want to decide what we do, how we do it, whom we interact with, when, and where. It doesn't necessarily mean that we want to be antisocial or work or live in a vacuum; instead, we simply want some control over our own lives and our own decisions. Think about how you perform best—when someone is micromanaging your every move or when you're given the freedom to make your own decisions?

Autonomy in the workplace exists on a continuum—from having none and being told exactly what to do, to working a typical job where sometimes you have autonomy and sometimes you don't, to what's now being referred to as a *results-only work environment* (ROWE).[4] First developed at Best Buy, the focus of ROWE, as the name implies, is to give all employees the freedom to do whatever they want, whenever they want, as long as the work gets done. Someone else still typically decides *what* you need to do, but you get to decide *how* to do it. Companies that have implemented ROWE have seen decreases in voluntary turnover, increases in productivity, and increases in worker engagement.

Some companies go to the extreme of almost complete autonomy. At companies such as manufacturer W. L. Gore[5] and video game developer and distributor Valve,[6] the organizational structure is completely flat, and employees are expected to decide what they want to work on, self-organize around projects that they find compelling (vote with their feet), manage their own commitments, and determine for themselves the best way they can serve the company. Employees at Gore and Valve are definitely directing their own lives, and their companies are known for their unique cultures and ongoing innovation.

Some companies look for a middle ground and carve out *autonomous time* for their employees to pursue their own interests. Many software companies run "hackathons," short 24-to 48-hour chunks of time where engineers can develop ideas unrelated to their day-to-day work (and eat pizza, drink beer, and not sleep). Google, taking a cue from early pioneers 3M and Hewlett-Packard (HP), offers its employees *20 percent time* — up to a day per week to be used on pet projects, wild ideas, and nonessential work. According to a talk[7] given by former Google executive Marissa Mayer in 2012, half of all new Google product launches at the time originated from 20-percent-time projects. And yet other companies, such as LinkedIn and Apple, are reportedly offering employees dedicated weeks or months to pursue independently conceived ideas that are deemed worthy of investment.

In our personal lives, we also have varying degrees of autonomy depending on the context and our stage in life. And when people lack autonomy in one area, they will often seek autonomous experiences in another so that they can experience that sense of control, of freedom, and of determining their own destiny. The popularity of video games, social games, and MMORPGs has demonstrated this.

Work Is All in Your Head

Probably the best-known story illustrating autonomy is from Mark Twain's *The Adventures of Tom Sawyer*, wherein Tom is tasked with painting his Aunt Polly's fence on a fine summer day. When his friends come to taunt him, he pretends that there's nothing in the world that he'd rather be doing. This, of course, piques their curiosity to the point where they're begging him to let them paint, too. By the end of the day, Tom has a legion of friends painting his fence, and they've paid him for the privilege. Mark Twain's point about this is incredibly astute. He states "that Work consists of whatever a body is obliged to do, and that Play consists of whatever a body is not obliged to do."

There's something really interesting going on here. For Tom, the act of painting the fence was work. For his friends, it was play. The nature of the task didn't change; they were doing the *exact same thing*, moving a paintbrush up and down a fence. What does this tell us about the difference between work and play? It tells us that the difference is completely in our heads, a "bit" that can be "flipped," that changes our perception of a task from something that we have to do into something that we want to do, and vice versa. Another way to look at it is the difference between being extrinsically motivated to do something (you're obligated owing to some external force) and being intrinsically motivated (you want to do it). And if you can figure out how to flip that bit, not by changing the task but by changing people's perception of the task, anything that is considered work can be turned into play—something that people want to do.

Mastery—"I Improve"

The second of the three motivators that we reference from SDT is *mastery* (which they refer to as "competence")—the innate desire that we have to be competent and to get better at things. Getting better at things is satisfying on a number of fronts. For some, it means that a job or task gets easier; for others, it means the psychic and possibly financial rewards that come from doing something that (1) we couldn't do before and (2) not everyone else can do.

Mastery requires a *growth mind-set*. According to Carol Dweck, a psychology professor at Stanford University, you can place people on a continuum based on their innate views on where ability comes from. Some people have a fixed mind-set, where they believe that basic qualities, such as intelligence and talent, are fixed traits that can't be changed. *Fixed mind-set* individuals dread any sort of failure because to them it's a negative reflection on their abilities, which are immutable. Because of this, they devote a lot of effort to trying to look smart and avoiding looking stupid—they won't engage in situations where they can fail, especially publicly. Growth mind-set individuals, on the other hand, believe that their basic abilities can be developed through dedication and hard work—that what they have right now is just the starting point. These people don't fear failure as much because they know that they can improve and that failure is a crucial part of the learning process.[8]

The road to mastery can be long and hard, and there will often be failure along the way, so people need to believe that they *can* get better and aren't limited by their current abilities. And many skills and tasks are *asymptotic*—for tasks such as playing golf or mastering a musical instrument, we can never reach perfection—we can always get better.

Purpose—"I Make a Difference"

I'm sure you've all had the experience: You create a great piece of work—a document, a presentation, or a set of plans for a new product. You worked hard on it, invested your time and your energy to make something great, and are proud of your work. The boss accepts your work, gives you a figurative or even a literal pat on the back, praises your work—and then, for whatever reason, your work is never used. The product is canceled, the deal is off, the company changes direction. Your work goes in a drawer, never to be seen again. You do good work you were trained for, you complete it on time, you turn it in, and you get paid. You should be happy, right?

Yet you're not happy, your motivation has dropped dramatically, and you're thinking that maybe you should get a new job. Why? Because there's something missing. And that something is *purpose*. To quote Steve Jobs, "We're here to put a dent in the universe. Otherwise, why else even be here?"[9] We all need to feel like we're making a difference and that our efforts and our existence have meaning.

In *The Upside of Irrationality*, Dan Ariely describes an experiment that he conducted that dramatically illustrates this. He recruited a group of students to build Lego robots. The students would be paid $2.00 for the first robot they built and then 11 cents less for each successive robot, so they'd receive $1.89 for the second robot, $1.78 for the third, and so on. At any time, when they decided they were done or that it wasn't worth it to build any more robots, they could quit and get paid. And at the beginning of each session, the research assistant explained to the student that the researchers used the same Legos for each student, so at some point before the next student showed up, the first student's robots would be disassembled and the Legos would be put back in the box.

There were two conditions in this experiment. One group

was assigned to the "meaningful" condition, in which when they were done building a robot it was placed in a box below the desk, awaiting disassembly before the next student arrived. Even though the students knew that their robots would be disassembled eventually, there was the illusion, a convenient fiction, that their robots would live forever and that there was therefore a purpose to their efforts.

In the second, "Sisyphean" condition (named for the Greek king Sisyphus, who was condemned to be forever rolling a rock up a hill, only to watch it roll back down), once a robot was completed, as the student was building the next one, the research assistant would slowly and visibly disassemble the just-completed robot and put the Legos back in the box. In this condition, the students were essentially building the same two robots over and over again. There was no illusion or convenient fiction here—their work was being taken apart right in front of their eyes, and it was clear that what they were doing had no purpose. It was like repeatedly digging a hole and then filling it back up again.

Can you guess which condition built more robots?

Students in the meaningful condition built an average of 10.6 robots, whereas those in the Sisyphean condition built 7.2 robots, 68 percent of what the students in the meaningful group built. In addition, when the payment per robot reached less than a dollar (half the initial payment), 65 percent of the students in the meaningful group kept working, whereas only 20 percent of those in the Sisyphean group did. The lack of purpose, the feeling that their work was useless, reduced their motivation.

People often wonder why others dedicate their time and energy to efforts such as contributing to open-source projects and writing and editing on Wikipedia for no financial gain. Now you know the answer—because there is a strong sense of purpose, of making a dent in the universe.

Progress—"I Achieve"

Harvard professor Teresa Amabile has been researching creative work for decades, and her most recent work is published in her book with Steven Kramer, *The Progress Principle: Using Small Wins to Ignite Joy, Engagement, and Creativity at Work.*[10] In this book, Amabile and Kramer describe a study they conducted that analyzed over 12,000 daily diary entries from 238 individuals spread across 7 companies and 26 project teams. Their goal was to understand the mental states of workers on a daily basis and see what events during the day correlated with motivation at work.

Through careful analysis of the diary entries, Amabile and Kramer discovered what they call the *progress principle*—that the event that correlated most highly with good days at work, with feeling motivated, was making progress toward a meaningful goal. When we think of progress, we typically think of major milestones or achievements, but the problem is that those are infrequent and by themselves aren't enough to sustain long-term performance and motivation—they're too far apart. The good news is that Amabile and Kramer's research uncovered that even *small wins* could have a significant, even disproportional impact on motivation and engagement.

Apparently, this news comes as a surprise to managers. In a separate survey of 669 managers from companies around the world, Amabile and Kramer asked them what managerial tools *they* thought motivated employees and gave them choices, including "support for making progress at work," "recognition for good work," "incentives," "interpersonal support," and "clear goals." Only 5 percent of the managers surveyed rated "support for making progress at work" as the number one motivator, and in fact, the vast majority of them rated it dead last. "Recognition for good work" was rated first. According to Amabile and

Kramer's research, recognition is certainly beneficial, but as they point out, without progress and achievement, there's not much to recognize.

Note also how our motivators are often intertwined—the fact that the progress needs to be toward something that employees find meaningful. They need to feel that there's a purpose to what they're doing and then to feel progress toward that purpose.

People respond well when they see that they are making progress on something they care about, whether in the workplace or in life. The lessons for engagement and motivation are fairly straightforward—make small wins *frequent*, *possible*, and *visible*.

Social Interaction—"I Connect with Others"

The final intrinsic motivator and the third from SDT is *social interaction* (which Deci and Ryan refer to as *relatedness*). We are inherently and innately social creatures. We want to connect, we want to interact, we want to affiliate, we want to care, we want to share, we want to be recognized, and we want to understand and be understood. The digital age has amplified our ability to do all of the above and made it global, real-time, all-the-time, and 140-character shallow or infinitely deep.

In the online consumer sphere, clearly *social* has taken off with Facebook, Twitter, and the like. Billions of people are spending hours each day interacting online about anything and everything. And following the natural progression of technology from the consumer sphere to the business sphere (the consumerization of IT that we talked about earlier), social is now making inroads into the workplace, with such products as Jive, Salesforce Chatter, and IBM Connections that enable sharing and collaborating around projects, products, and customers.

The desire for validation and recognition from others is

another huge driver of our behavior. We post status updates and hope that people "Like" them, we share photos and obsessively check to see what people have to say about them, and we write reviews on product sites and hope that people mark them as helpful. What's the point of doing these things if no one else can see them?

We also look to others to figure out appropriate behavior. From tip jars, to watching to see which fork people use at dinner, to looking at a newsfeed of activity on a social network—seeing what others are doing, the *social norm*, gives us cues that tell us how to behave, what possible actions should be, and what's expected of us. Studies have shown us that people are more likely to adhere to the social norms of others "like" them. That *likeness* can be in the form of personal or identity commonalities (such as race, interests, etc.) but also situational or contextual commonalities. Your customers, partners, and employees all exist in a shared social context with each other, so if you can establish the social norms in their respective communities, you have a powerful tool to motivate high-value activity and loyalty.

Remember in Chapter 1 when we talked about the four tiers of loyalty? The bottom two tiers, inertia loyalty and mercenary loyalty, were characterized by a transactional relationship between the business and the consumer. And if the consumer could get a better transaction elsewhere and wasn't too lazy to move, he'd leave you. The upper tiers, though, true loyalty and cult loyalty, were about creating social relationships between the business and the consumer that transcended the market norms and made customers much less likely to defect. And by *social*, we don't mean that they "Liked" your company page on Facebook; we mean that there's a real relationship, real engagement, that bonds the customer to your business.

Piece of Cake?

So it's easy, right? Give your participants autonomy, "flip the bit" between work and play so that your participants want to engage, make sure that they have a growth mind-set and a never-ending path to mastery, give them a meaningful purpose to work for, provide them with clear and frequent indicators of progress, and enable them to do it all in a social context.

Okay, it actually sounds kind of daunting. But never fear—the whole point of Loyalty 3.0 is to use the big data being generated by your constituents as they interact with you and the data-driven motivational techniques of gamification to be able to do this and do it automatically and at scale. We'll see examples of companies doing exactly this in Chapters 5, 6, and 7.

I Just Work for a Paycheck

As we mentioned earlier, not all jobs lend themselves to some or all of these intrinsic motivators. If your job is making pizza at Evan's Pizza Shack, an algorithmic job, you likely:

- Don't have much autonomy or control over how you do your work.
- Have mastered how to make pizza and so have no way to grow or improve.
- Don't feel like your work has a greater purpose, other than to provide you a paycheck so that you can survive and pursue your other interests.
- Don't feel like you're progressing toward a meaningful goal.
- May or may not enjoy the social interaction with your customers and peers.

And within the boundaries of this job, there might not be much flexibility to change this. In these kinds of cases, the solution is to use extrinsic motivators, which we'll discuss more in Chapter 4. But first we need to understand the second fuel source for Loyalty 3.0—big data.

Building Loyalty 3.0

- Human motivation is one of the foundational components of Loyalty 3.0.

- There are two kinds of motivators: intrinsic (from within) and extrinsic (an external force).

- Intrinsic motivators aren't necessarily better than extrinsic motivators. A good motivation system may have both intrinsic and extrinsic elements.

- The five key intrinsic motivators are

    o *Autonomy*—I control.

    o *Mastery*—I improve.

    o *Purpose*—I make a difference.

    o *Progress*—I achieve.

    o *Social interaction*—I connect with others.

- Intrinsic motivators are often better suited for heuristic tasks, whereas extrinsic motivators are better suited for algorithmic tasks.

CHAPTER 3

The Next Big Thing Is Big Data

In Chapter 2 we took a deep dive into the world of motivation. Now we switch gears away from human behavior and into big data, the second fuel source in our Loyalty 3.0 equation (Figure 3.1). Remember, true loyalty is about building relationships, which starts with getting to know one another. Big data enables businesses to know their customers, employees, and partners in unprecedented ways. We're going to take a fast survey of the big-data landscape so that you have a functional understanding and a vocabulary to use. Then in Chapter 4 we'll see how we can apply "gamification" to the mix—to consume big data and use it to motivate participants to be more active and loyal.

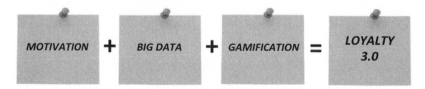

Figure 3.1 THE LOYALTY 3.0 EQUATION.

What Is Big Data and Where Does It Come From?

Now, in the grand schema of things (Get it? No? You will!), data is hardly a new thing. In the course of human history, the availability of electronic data covers a small sliver of time. *Big data*, however, has arrived more recently. Traditional data, such as customer or employee records about you, where you live, what you've purchased, and how you've performed, is "old news," stored in structured databases and made available to anyone with the appropriate access, the right querying tools, and a *schema* (i.e., an architectural diagram or schematic) of the database. *Big data* refers to the explosion in the size, amount, and form of information available around any one individual, organization, or event. It comes from an increasingly wide variety of sources; is assembled in a variety of forms, some structured and processed and some unstructured and unprocessed; and is present in heretofore unimagined quantities.

For years, companies had a standard, structured customer record with name, address, phone numbers, e-mail address, and perhaps some historical transactional data. They might have supplemented this with some externally sourced marketing information, including interests derived through magazine subscriptions or expected behaviors inferred from where you lived or your socioeconomic class. Over the years, this record has grown to contain more and more data—but still in a standard, structured format.

Fast-forward to now, and the expansion of computing power, mobile devices, and other new data-input streams has added another massive layer of available information. Huge new streams of unstructured data have become available to tap into because nearly everything we're doing is mediated by technology and therefore able to generate data. Among the many sources are "clickstreams," Internet Protocol (IP) addresses, Global Positioning System, (GPS) locations, mobile phone usage, online shopping patterns, social networks, radio-frequency identification (RFID) chips, sensors and connected devices, mentions in blog posts, customer feedback, and other "public" information you create or read from the Internet. These and almost unlimited other sources have greatly expanded the amount of data being generated and available for businesses to consume. As Massachusetts Institute of Technology (MIT) researchers Andrew McAfee and Erik Brynjolfsson put it in a recent *Harvard Business Review* article,[1] "Each of us is now a walking data generator."

The data are (1) unlikely to be in one place, (2) unlikely to be owned or controlled by one organization, (3) not managed through traditional "structured" database tools, and (4) gigantic—it is referred to as *big data*. Analyst firm Gartner defined *big data* as follows: "Big data in general is defined as high volume, velocity and variety information assets that demand cost-effective, innovative forms of information processing for enhanced insight and decision making."[2] Or to summarize, there are three V's—volume, velocity, and variety—that serve to delineate big data from traditional data.

How Can We Use Big Data?

The upshot of big data in the business-to-individual relationship is pretty simple: With big data, a business can learn a lot about *what you do, where you do it, when you do it,* and *what you like*. Another way to look at it is that your constituents are raising their hands and telling you things about themselves, implicitly and explicitly, all the time through their interactions with you. Big-data collection and processing tools enable you to listen and react.

Just How Big Is Big Data?

The explosion of computing power, the power and low cost of network and mass-storage devices, and the increase in data-generating systems all have contributed to the current size and volume of big data. There is no real finite limit or definition of the *size* of big data. To give you a sense of the scale people generally think about in the big-data context, one estimate of the size of the databases at Walmart alone is 2.5 *petabytes* of data[3]—the equivalent of 167 times the books in the U.S. Library of Congress. A petabyte is 1 million gigabytes, which is roughly equivalent to 20 million file cabinets worth of text. Online commerce giant eBay processes 50 petabytes *per day* of activity data as its users search, bid on, and navigate through its site.[4]

Add it all up, and the total amount of new data estimated to be created *each day* is 2.5 *exabytes*[5]—1,000 times the size of all that Walmart has in storage. In fact, most corporations each have more data stored than the Library of Congress. Perhaps more tellingly, the volume of business data worldwide across all companies is estimated to double every 1.2 years,[6] with new data-generation rates growing 40 percent annually.[7] According to Eric Schmidt, chairman of Google, between the dawn of civilization and 2003, 5 exabytes of information were created. Now we're generating that amount every two days.[8]

The applications in marketing are numerous and straightforward—from targeting advertisements and offers to optimizing merchandise layout, e-mail marketing, and conversion funnels. Big data also reaches into the core functions of a business to help manage research and development, manufacturing, and supply-chain and other activities. And as we'll see, big data also can help considerably with employee and partner engagement.

Of course, one obvious question is "how?" How does big data help us do these things?

At this point, a heavy technical explanation of how big data works or how it is analyzed isn't important—that's better left to IT professionals, data scientists, and certified number crunchers. Instead, we'll give a high-level summary of some of the big-data analyses and the kinds of outcomes they can produce and then provide a short overview of some of the more prominent big-data processing tools. Again, the point here is to build a vocabulary and to know what questions to ask—not to become an expert yourself.

Here are some of the important forms of big-data collection and analysis:

- **Cluster analysis.** Cluster analysis is a classification technique that partitions a diverse set of objects into smaller groups so that objects in the same cluster are more similar to each other than to objects in other clusters. The key thing to note is that these groupings or similarities are not known in advance. For instance, ask a random group of people their feelings on science fiction on a scale from −5 (hate it) to +5 (love it). Ask those same people their feelings on chocolate with the same −5 to +5 scale. Plot out all their responses on a graph, with people who love science fiction and chocolate at the upper right and those who hate them both at the bottom left. Are the responses evenly distributed throughout the graph, or do you see clusters occurring? Each of those clusters is a group of individuals who have similar feelings about science fiction and chocolate, and that information now can be used to communicate with them in a way they're more likely to respond to. In a retail scenario, for instance, if there was a distinctive cluster of people in the upper right who liked science fiction and chocolate, whenever anyone checked out with Star Wars DVDs, you might offer them some chocolate as an upsell.

- **A/B testing (also called split testing).** This is a technique in which a control group (A) is compared with a test group (B) to determine what treatments (changes) will improve a given objective, for example, a marketing response or an engagement rate—typically referred to as a *conversion rate*. Suppose that you're trying to determine whether an offer, the timing of an offer, or even how it's presented on your website is effective. With A/B testing, you can try several approaches to see which one delivers the highest conversion rate, that is, the result you want. Conversion can be any *success condition* and might include registering, making a purchase, or even something as simple as pressing a button to go to the next step in a flow. *Multivariate testing* is a variation of A/B testing that enables a business to run several A/B tests at the same time. The size of the sample (number of tests) required depends on the number of variables being tested and the confidence desired in the results.

  On websites, companies often A/B test the copy, placement, color, and size of their "call to action" buttons, which might have text such as "Join now," "Buy now," or "Learn more" on them, to see which one results in the most click-throughs (conversions). While people can have opinions and guesses as to the right answer, A/B testing can objectively determine the optimal solution.

- **Crowdsourcing** is the outsourcing of work to a distributed group of people who aren't known ahead of time, aka "the crowd." There are numerous forms of crowdsourcing, typi-

cally reflecting the nature of the work being outsourced—
opinions, piece work, computing power, ideas, and even
funding. Some well-known examples include

o **Threadless.** Started in 2000, Threadless is an online
community of millions of artists who design T-shirts.
Here's the interesting part: Every week the community
members submit hundreds, sometimes even thousands
of T-shirt designs, and then they provide feedback and
vote on each other's submissions. At the end of the
week, Threadless staff reviews the top-ranked submissions and, based on the score and user feedback, se-
lects around 10 designs to print onto T-shirts and other
clothing items, which are then sold via the website and
at their retail store in Chicago. Designers whose submissions are printed receive cash and Threadless gift
cards as compensation. So here you have a company
whose content (the designs) is being crowdsourced,
product offering is being crowdsourced (via voting
and feedback), sales forecasting is being crowdsourced
(again via voting and feedback), and even marketing
is being crowdsourced (winning designers spread the
word to get people to buy their creations).

o **CrowdFlower.** CrowdFlower enables businesses to
crowdsource work tasks to millions of workers around
the world. Examples of the kinds of microtasks that can
be crowdsourced include image moderation (Is there
anything offensive in this picture?), sentiment analysis
(Is this tweet saying something positive or negative?),
categorization (What genre does this video belong
to?), and content creation (Write a short article about
loyalty). For businesses with ever-growing amounts of
data that need to be processed by humans (such as

Facebook, which needs millions of photos moderated), services such as CrowdFlower enable them to achieve scale. One of the benefits of having a large workforce such as CrowdFlower's is that you can have multiple people perform the same task and then use the consensus "vote" to determine the correct answer (i.e., if two of three workers think this image is offensive, only then do you label it as offensive). In addition, over time, the data about how often workers complete tasks on time and how well (with the consensus vote) can be used to create a "reputation" for each worker that can be used to offer her more and better opportunities.

o   **Stock market.** Stock prices are an indicator of the market's collective belief in the future potential of a business. They're the aggregate of hundreds of thousands of opinions being voiced by traders with their trades, at microsecond speeds. What should IBM's stock price be right now? No individual knows, but "the crowd" does. The winners in the stock market are often the ones who can best process the big data that sets the context for the market (e.g., economics, politics, news, customer sentiment, etc.) and who can act on it the fastest.

- **Predictive modeling** refers to a set of mathematical modeling techniques created to best predict an outcome. It goes farther than clustering—rather than stop at a group with similar behaviors and attributes, it predicts what that group might *do* under certain circumstances based on current and historical facts and data. Predictive models are used, for instance, to predict the weather in a given location from a wide assortment of direct and indirect causal factors. In the consumer space, a predictive model might estimate the likelihood of a customer engaging in or joining a program, staying with a program, or "churning" away from it. Like the weather forecast, the analysis is based on a broad assortment of direct and indirect causal factors and correlations with other behaviors. These models also can predict the likelihood of success of a cross-sell or upsell opportunity. Employers also use predictive modeling to help predict employee churn and turnover or even to predict who their top and bottom performers will be.

- **Sentiment analysis** analyzes mostly "soft," unstructured communication streams to try to pick up customer, employee, or partner sentiment on a subject, a product, or other item being analyzed. Sentiment analysis applies natural-language processing (using computers to understand human language) and other analytic techniques to large quantities of source text material, including blogs and other social media, to identify and extract subjective information. The analysis starts with simple keyword location (if the word *great* is in the blog, then it's probably saying something good) and expand from there (What if the user was posting about the "great big screwup" the company made. Uh oh. Time to get more sophisticated.). So-called *buzz analyzers* attempt to identify patterns of written sentiment on a product or a campaign. They examine how much is being expressed and what kind of sentiment or *polarity*—positive, negative, or neutral comments—is being expressed. More sophisticated analyzers try to figure out the degree and strength of the sentiment. "These new Burton snowboards are really awesome" would send a strong sentiment signal, especially if it appeared all over the Internet. Consumer marketers use sentiment analysis to determine how different customer segments are reacting to their products and actions. Likewise, strong positive sentiment in internal communication is a gauge of engagement with an employer.

- **Stream processing** refers to the continuous and real-time analysis of data streams from a variety of sources. Stream processing works together with all the techniques mentioned to adapt and modify a digital experience *in real time* in order to provide tailored interactions depending on behavior, location, context, or any other variable. Real-time fraud detection and algorithm-based high-frequency securities trading are examples of stream-processing applications. And as we'll see in Chapter 4, so is "gamification."

- **Outlier detection and similarity search.** Often you want to find the outliers, the deviations from the norm, as in the case of fraud detection, clinical trials, voting activities, and manufacturing defects. These outliers can help you to identify problems, lend insight to your product-design process, and expose bad behavior. By feeding big data from various sources into machine-learning systems that can process them, businesses can find correlations that manual human analysis would never identify and surface the outliers. Conversely, big data also provides the data to locate the other objects that are most similar to an object of interest—for instance, "Find other shoes that look like these," "Find other patients with similar symptoms," and "Find other songs that sound like this."

- **Cohort analysis.** A *cohort* is a group of people who share a common characteristic over a certain period of time. By dividing users into cohorts, businesses can compare the relative value of each cohort. An example of a cohort that's relevant to an online retailer would be the source of the customer—"all the customers who came from a Google search," "all the customers who came from Twitter," "all the customers who came via referral," and so on. With each customer assigned to a cohort and the data about each customer's overall spend, the retailer now has the ability to see which sources provide the most valuable customers. With this knowledge, the retailer can optimize its marketing spending to get the most bang for its buck.

Another cohort that companies often use is the date of customer acquisition ("everyone who joined in December 2012," "everyone who joined in January 2013," and so on). Combined with the overall spend of each customer, businesses then can see if the quality of their customers is increasing or decreasing over time. In addition, if the business is making changes to its product, service, or experience, time-based cohorts enable a business to make an apples-to-apples comparison to see if the changes are having any material impact on its success.

Is There Anyone Out There?

There are millions of computers at homes and business around the world sitting idle at any point in time, doing nothing while they wait for people to come use them. What if you could harness all that idle computing power? What if you could take a big computing job, one that you'd typically need a supercomputer to run, and break it into millions of small pieces that you could distribute to individual machines, have them process the pieces, and then send you back the results? You could process huge quantities of data more quickly, efficiently, and cheaply than ever before.

The folks at Search for Extraterrestrial Intelligence (SETI) figured this out. In their search for alien life, they have radio telescopes listening for radio signals from space.

The computing power required to process all the radio-signal data that SETI is collecting is enormous. Rather than try to acquire gigantic supercomputers (and the money to buy them!) to process the data, SETI created the SETI@home project, which asks for volunteers to run a screensaver on their computers. During the computer's "idle" time, the screensaver pulls down a small piece of the data, processes it, and then uploads the results back to SETI. By crowdsourcing computing power and innovating new ways for people to contribute to big causes, the SETI@home project is able to process a big data set that it would never be able to make a dent in on its own.

Want to contribute your computing time to curing disease, studying global warming, or discovering pulsars? Or maybe you want to set up your own "grid computing" project to solve a big-data business problem? If your answer to either question is "Yes," check out the Berkeley Open Infrastructure for Network Computing (BOINC) project at the University of California Berkeley—it's open-source software for doing exactly that.

Crunching the Numbers

As you start exploring the world of big data, you'll run across some of the tools that people use to store it, crunch it, and visualize it. These tools range from relatively straightforward business-intelligence tools that provide querying, reporting, and digital dashboards to more advanced data-mining tools (*data mining* is an umbrella term for an assortment of statistical-analysis tools that search for patterns in large amounts of data). Many of these tools work only with in-house, structured databases or data warehouses, in contrast to the large, unstructured data sets that are currently being generated, and therefore aren't suitable for many of today's web-scale businesses. To address this, the tech industry has created a new set of large-scale processing systems for highly distributed data from multiple, decentralized, and often unstructured data sources. Some of the ones that are good to know about include:

- **Not Only SQL (NoSQL).** This is the blanket term used for a new class of modern, web-scale databases that have to deal with huge amounts of data. Structured Query Language (SQL) is a standard programming language for getting information out of and putting information into databases. Typical SQL databases exhibit certain characteristics that developers have required over the years: They use the relational model that includes ACID (atomicity, consistency, isolation, durability—a set of properties that guarantee that database transactions are processed reliably), and they have a fixed schema. These properties are what enable your credit-card company and stock broker to run their mission-critical systems and ensure that no data is lost and that they are always up to date and consistent, 24/7, around the world.

  Today's high-volume consumer Internet sites such as Facebook and Twitter don't always need these mission-critical properties. What they need instead is a system that scales easily to handle their huge volume of big data and runs on commodity hardware. Hence NoSQL was born. In practice, most companies are running a combination of SQL and NoSQL databases depending on the needs of each particular application. Some NoSQL systems that you might hear about include Cassandra (developed by Facebook for inbox search), Voldemort (developed by Linked In), Dynamo (developed by Amazon), MongoDB, and

HBase. Many of these are open source and have active developer communities that are continually enhancing them.

- **Hadoop.** Named after a toy elephant in the household of Doug Cutting, one of its creators, Hadoop is an open-source free software framework for processing huge data sets across a distributed hardware system. Its development was inspired by Google, one of the pioneers in dealing with web-scale data, and the tools the company built to process and store that data, including MapReduce and Google File System (GFS). Hadoop is used heavily today by Yahoo!, Facebook, and many others for an assortment of tasks. If you're interested in using Hadoop for your own data analysis, you can either set it up yourself on your own dedicated machines or deploy it "in the cloud" by using an "infrastructure as a service provider" such as Amazon's EC2. Sensing a market opportunity, there are also several new companies that have formed to help businesses get up and running, analyzing their data quickly, including Birst, Cloudera, Platfora, Hadapt, MapR, Hortonworks, and others.

Beyond these data crunchers (and there are many others), there is an assortment of *visualization* tools that also can help the big-data user. Visualization tools enable users to make sense of the big data, identify patterns, and derive some insight that ultimately can lead to action and a business result. Tools such as the statistical computing and graphic language R are used often by data scientists and engineers to analyze and visualize their data, whereas business users leverage visualization software provided by companies like Tableau Software that provide interfaces and displays designed for business users (see Figure 3.2).

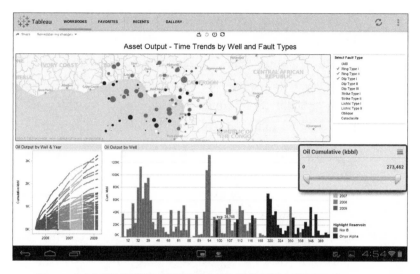

Figure 3.2 DATA VISUALIZATION FROM TABLEAU SOFTWARE.
Source: Tableau Software, Inc. © 2013.

Big Data in the Consumer Space

When you're trying to sell more, anything that helps you to get the right message to the right person at the right time is worth its weight in gold. Here are some of the ways that businesses are using big data to drive their top-line revenues:

- **Microsegmentation.** For years, companies divided their markets into segments based on easily identified traits such as gender, ZIP code, and age. As more data became readily available, such as income, psychographics, and purchase data, companies were able to refine those segments to better address the needs of their customers. The truth of the matter is, though, that no two people are alike—we are each a "segment of one." Big data takes the existing data that can be collected and inferred about a consumer and then supplements it with online browsing behavior, shopping patterns, social-networking activity, mobile access, and much more data based on actual user behavior to create microsegments. Do you remember when Amazon.com was the same store for everyone? It seems hard to believe that it was ever that way. Today it's a different store for every single person who visits — because of big data and real-time microsegmentation.

- **Targeted advertising and cross-selling.** Microsegmentation also enables businesses to craft the "perfect" cross-sell/upsell offer to close or expand a sale in real time. Based on everything they know about the individual shopper, others like them that might exhibit similar behavior patterns, and the current context (Is the user in a physical store? Did the user come to the website from a marketing e-mail?), businesses are able to dynamically and automatically generate compelling offers that will increase shopping-cart conversion and average order size.

- **In-store behavior analysis.** Real-time navigation analysis can provide fascinating insight into customer behavior. Tracking motion through physical stores with shopping-cart transponders or video surveillance or passively monitoring the location of mobile phones has helped retailers to enhance their offerings and refine store layout and product positioning. Naturally, though, in the Internet age, it isn't just physical movements that are being monitored; marketers and retailers constantly tune into customer movements through their websites to determine interest and intent. Unlike in the real world, online retailers can easily detect browsing, sharing, where shoppers arrived from, video watching, and abandoned carts, all of which enable them to refine their marketing messages and channels, their offers, their product mix, and their conversion rates.

- **Real-time pricing optimization.** Driven by sales history, weather, seasonality, available inventory, time of day, data about the customer, and the overall economy (among others) as inputs, retailers can change their prices dynamically to reflect demand. Just as the airlines dynamically price today to optimize their seat utilization, any business can leverage big data to optimize its inventory and pricing. Amazon and other large Internet retailers are already doing this.

- **Social-media monitoring.** This is part of a larger trend toward what's known as *social customer relationship management* (SCRM), where companies monitor their customer relationships, check the "market pulse," and collect data from their customers using social-media channels. These channels include Facebook and Twitter, as well as conventional blogs and message boards. The business seeks to learn from these channels and add to the conversation where it can, recognizing that the collective message is really owned by the community. The emphasis here is on listening, not on using the channel as an outbound marketing channel. Tools and social-media dashboards such as HootSuite, SocialMention, and salesforce.com's Radian6 monitor these channels to capture messages, detect sentiment, and classify messages and meanings for use by different departments in an organization.

- **Recommendation engines.** Businesses can use big data to predict things you might be interested in. When you're looking at a product on Amazon and the site shows you "Customers Who Bought This Item Also Bought," the company is using its giant collection of everyone's purchasing behavior to recommend products that you're likely to want to buy as well. When you're on Netflix and the site recommends a movie to you, the company is basing its recommendation on the ratings you've given other movies, what you've actually rented, and the viewing history of everyone else on the site. And when you're creating a custom station in Pandora, you seed it with a few of your favorite artists whose "genome" Pandora knows, and it can then find other music of a similar type. Then, by consistently indicating whether you like or dislike songs, the company is able to refine its recommendations and continuously predict other songs and artists you might like and play them for you.

Big Data in the Employee Space

As we saw from many of the examples referenced earlier, big data has clearly had a huge impact on many aspects of the business-to-consumer experience, including sales, marketing, and customer relationship management (CRM). Where it surprisingly hasn't had as big an impact yet is in the business-to-employee relationship. Mark my words, this is going to be the next big opportunity for big data.

Think about it—Facebook knows more about your employees than you do, Amazon knows more about your employees than you do, and Netflix knows more about your employees than you do. Yet these people spend the bulk of their waking lives with you, doing work for you, in systems and structures that are tracking every piece of data about their performance, their skills, and their progress toward goals. The value that you as an employer derive from these individuals is orders of magnitude more than what any of the companies listed earlier do, and yet these companies know more than you do, and they use their big data about your employees to create personalized, relevant experiences that drive engagement and loyalty. There is a massive opportunity for businesses to begin to capture and use the big data being generated by their employees as they work in order to understand them better and to motivate and engage them through data.

Let's take a look at some of the ways that big data can be used to make work better for both employees and managers.

Employee Hiring: An End to Hunches

The variability in the hiring process between companies and even within a company is tremendous. Different managers look for different things, have different hot and cold buttons, weight attributes (such as academics and experience) differently, and have different levels of training in how to interview and identify key traits, both positive and negative. To a large degree, hiring is still based on hunches, biases, and "gut feel." Yet it's probably one of the most crucial jobs that a manager performs—great hires can make a company and poor ones can break it, so why aren't we bringing more rigor to this process? We already have a large pool of employees, we know how they're performing, and we know (or can learn) certain details about them. Can we correlate certain employee traits to good performance based on our existing employees and then test for those traits in the hiring process? Figure 3.3 summarizes some of the problems companies face and suggests some possible solutions.

Some companies are starting to do just that. Xerox Corp. reportedly cut attrition in its call centers by 20 percent by ignoring its conventional wisdom and assumptions that experience was the most important factor when hiring.[9] Working with Evolv, Inc., a Silicon Valley start-up that "utilizes big-data predictive analytics and machine learning to optimize the performance of global hourly workforces," Xerox was able to build a model of an ideal call-center worker that included such attri-

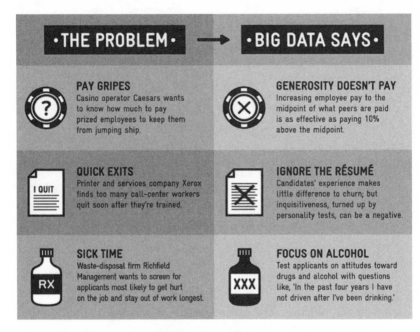

Figure 3.3 BIG DATA IN EMPLOYEE HIRING.
Reprinted by permission of *The Wall Street Journal.* Copyright ©
2012 Dow Jones & Company, Inc. All Rights Reserved Worldwide.
License number: 3112720114387.

butes as "being creative but not overly inquisitive" and then use
that model to construct tests to use during the hiring process.
These tests score candidates against the model and give Xerox
data-driven confidence in its hiring decisions. Call centers are
clearly algorithmic jobs, and it remains to be seen whether this
"algorithmic hiring" will work for heuristic jobs as well.

The practice is growing quickly. Companies such as
Kenexa, now a part of IBM, tested 30 million applicants in
2011 for thousands of clients. And according to Gartner, spending on "talent management" software rose 15 percent to $3.8
billion in 2011, with major IT firms such as IBM, Oracle, and
SAP adding talent management to their offerings.[10]

Workforce Analytics

Employees are using a multitude of systems inside the workplace: sales force automation, social collaboration, and learning management, to name just a few. Each of these can contribute information about a specific facet of the employee's skills and performance to a comprehensive "360-degree view" of that employee—I often think of it as an employee "baseball card." With their baseball cards, employees can see where they're strong and where they need improvement. With a collection of baseball cards—employees and their live statistics—managers can field better teams and make the work experience better for their employees. Some of the interesting analytics and insight that we can generate with this big data on employee activity include:

- **Progress toward goals.** The number one question employees have at any company is, "How am I doing right now?" As we'll see in the next section, historically this question gets answered in a once-a-year review process that no one really cares for. With big data, we can give employees real-time statistics that show them how they're doing in relation to all their measurable goals. We can also use this data in aggregate to identify stars and underperformers on the team and compare business units against each other.

- **"Live" performance reviews.** The Department of Labor reports that 64 percent of working Americans leave their jobs because they don't feel appreciated.[11] More specifically, a recent poll by talent management company Taleo (now part of Oracle) found that four of five workers are dissatisfied with performance reviews[12]; even harsher still was another study, published in *The Psychological Bulletin*, suggesting that 38 percent of performance reviews ended up in decreased employee performance.[13] Why do you think this is? I'd posit that it's because the feedback that is given is poor and because it has missed all the nuances and individual ups and downs of the prior year and so necessarily can only be broad and not very useful. In addition, it's given only once a year, so employees have no way to evolve and grow in the interim. Finally, they're subject to the same hunches, biases, and gut feelings that hiring is and so can feel unfair.

With big data, you have real-time, system-generated metrics on how your employees are performing, and everyone knows exactly where they stand at any point in time. If you supplement the system-generated metrics with a culture of continuous peer feedback and recognition (which you are also capturing), then you truly have a real-time, live, instant performance review that consists of complementary human and system data at your fingertips for every employee.

- **Employee skills.** Everyone wants to know "who can do what" inside a company so that the company can always put the best individuals on a job and find internal expertise when needed, but that knowledge is often inaccessible. Big data can take a mix of what employees say about themselves ("I'm a great JavaScript programmer"), what others say about them ("She's a great JavaScript programmer"), and what objective measures say ("She has passed the Advanced JavaScript test"). We'll discuss this more in Chapter 7 when we look at Loyalty 3.0 examples in the employee space and discuss reputation systems.

- **Employee influence networks.** How does information travel inside your company? Who are the connectors, the nodes, and the influencers? Who are the people who bridge the various groups inside your company? Use big data to track how your employees are connected and how information spreads across your company.

- **Benchmarking.** How are your employees doing relative to one another? One branch versus another? Your company versus others in the same field? Once you start measuring, you can start benchmarking. And while your managers and employees might not care if you tell them their score on some metric is a 10, they will definitely care when you tell them that your biggest competitor has a 15.

- **Predictive analytics.** We can use this data to predict such things as which employees are at risk for leaving, who are going to be top and bottom performers, who is likely to get injured and file for workers' compensation, and even such things as whether products will ship on time.

- **Personalization.** The same way that Facebook, Amazon, and Netflix personalize their user experiences for consumers, applications used at work can start personalizing their user experiences based on an employee's past history, skills, progress toward goals, and current context.

Big Data, Big Problems?

Everybody is talking about big data. It's clear, though, that not everyone knows what to do about it. There are legacy technology systems to deal with, potential regulatory issues concerning privacy, a lack of skilled workers who know how to handle big data, and a general lack of clarity around the question of what to do with it. And as the size of the data we collect grows ever larger, it's going to become more and more challenging to find the signal in the noise. While it's easy to collect data, the challenge is—and always has been—figuring out the right questions to ask, ensuring that you're collecting the right data to answer the questions, and then making sure that the answers are timely, actionable, and can inform and drive change toward a desired business result. Even before big data, this was the case. The three V's of big data just amplify the problem.

That said, the potential for big data across retail, communications, health care, entertainment, financial services, employee performance management, and numerous other fields is immense, so big data can't be ignored. And whether you're a big or a small company, the tools for capturing and analyzing big data are becoming cheaper and more accessible by the day. Now is the time to start understanding it, experimenting with it, and leveraging it to drive a competitive advantage for your business.

What's Next?

You've seen how businesses are capturing, analyzing, clustering, crowdsourcing, predicting, benchmarking, modeling, segmenting, and targeting using big data. What we haven't seen yet is how to use big data to *motivate*—and that's exactly where we're going next, with gamification.

Building Loyalty 3.0

- Big data refers to the enormous and rapidly increasing body of data available for any one individual, organization, or event. As the saying goes, "Each of us is now a walking data generator."

- The volume of business data available is estimated to double every 1.2 years.

- Among other things, big data supports cluster analysis, A/B testing, predictive modeling, crowdsourcing, sentiment analysis, and real-time stream processing.

- In the consumer space, big data supports microsegmentation, in-store (and on-site) behavior analysis, and real-time pricing optimization. Completing a cycle, these activities not only are supported by but also *support* big data by creating new data in their own right.

- Big data will be used increasingly in the employee sphere to drive hiring, show progress and status, appraise skills, predict performance, and more.

- Big-data initiatives can be difficult, but the benefits are worth it. Now is the time to get started.

CHAPTER 4

Gamification— The Engine of Loyalty 3.0

If motivation and big data had a love child, its name would be *gamification*. Don't let the *game* in the name fool you, because this is serious stuff, and it's been around in various forms for as long as there have been people. In simple terms, gamification takes the motivational techniques that video game designers have used for years to motivate players and uses them in nongame contexts. These techniques include, but aren't limited to, such things as giving users goals to accomplish, awarding them with badges, engaging them with competition, encouraging them to collaborate in teams, giving them status by leveling them up, and enabling them to earn points. Other phrases that you might recognize that also can be used to describe gamification include:

- Measure and motivate
- Recognition and rewards
- Loyalty
- Reputation
- Guiding and amplifying high-value activity

I don't think that anyone would disagree that these are good things, and smart businesses have been doing many of them very effectively for years. If you boil them down to their essence, the core theme that runs through these concepts, and the core definition of *gamification*, is *motivating people through data*. What kind of data? Big data about user activity.

One way that you can use user-activity data to motivate people is by enabling them to visualize and derive some insight from it, which will hopefully motivate behavior change. This concept (some would call it a movement) even has a name—the *quantified self*—whose purpose is to derive self-knowledge though self-tracking. By capturing and analyzing data about your weight, sleep patterns, computer usage, spending, athletic performance, or anything else, you can better understand those aspects of your life and what affects them and then use that knowledge to motivate behavior change. In the past, this required a great deal of manual work—you had to do all the data collection and analysis yourself—logging every meal, entering your weight into a spreadsheet every day, and so on. This is no longer the case—technology has automated and simplified much of this data collection through sensors, mobile apps, and hooks into existing software systems.

Some examples of quantified self products include:

- **RescueTime**, a desktop application and web-browser plugin that monitors how you're spending your time on your computer and how much of it is productive versus unproductive

- **Fitbit**, a suite of products that includes an activity monitor, website, mobile application, and scale that enable users to track steps, distance, calories, stair climbing, sleep cycles, weight, and more

- **Mint**, a website that gives you insight into your finances and how you're spending and saving money

- **RunKeeper**, a mobile application that tracks your runs, walks, or bike rides and includes statistics such as pace, distance, time, routes, heart rate, and personal bests

Another way that you can use this data to motivate people is to supplement the visualization with goals to work toward, real-time feedback as they progress, rewards for their achievements, and a community of people to compete and collaborate with. This is gamification, and companies such as Khan Academy, USA Network, and Nike are using it successfully to motivate behavior in fan-engagement programs, training, job performance, education, and health care. In Part 2 we'll take a closer look at how several companies are using gamification as a key part of their Loyalty 3.0 strategies to engage customers and fans, motivate learning and skill development, and engage and motivate employees.

What they're doing isn't new. You've seen the different colored belts in karate that give students milestones to work toward and a visible way of displaying their status in a community. We've even seen these "belts" used in the workplace as part of the Six Sigma methodology, made famous by General Electric (GE) in the 1990s. Boy Scout badges and medals in the military fill similar functions, and Loyalty 1.0 programs have used primitive gamification components since the beginning—with points to be accumulated, tiers to reach, and rewards to be earned. Finally, the world of work is full of gamification, with participants "leveling up" to better jobs, competing and collaborating, and working to achieve major milestones and reap rewards. As you can see, these *gamification mechanics*, which include leveling up, goal setting, competition, and others that we'll describe later in the chapter, have been around for years.

So why this new field, then, called *gamification*? What has changed in recent years is the availability of big data that enables businesses to use these motivational techniques at scale, in an automated fashion, around behaviors that were previously inaccessible. Streams of big data on user activity are sent to the business, and in real-time, the business feeds that data to a *gamification engine* that processes the data, feeds it through a set of rules, updates all the necessary statistics, and then responds to users with real-time feedback and other data-driven motivational techniques.

Gamification's goals are the business's goals, whatever they may be: better learning, increased performance, more page views, more sales, increased collaboration, or anything else a business might want to drive. And it accomplishes them by processing the big data that users generate as they interact with various systems and then using that data to motivate, engage, and drive action.

This Is Not a Game: The Difference Between Games and Gamification

When hearing the word *gamification*, the first thing that jumps to mind for many people is the creation of stand-alone games — both casual and social games such as Farmville, Minecraft, and Angry Birds or more "hardcore" games such as World of Warcraft, Call of Duty, and Portal. These are clearly all games, experiences cut from whole cloth, whose sole purpose is to entertain. Creating successful games is hard, as thousands of failed game studios will tell you, and it's a hit-driven business with a fickle audience, just like any other entertainment medium.

Since the context of the conversation is generally about business, people understand that gamification isn't about entertainment but about achieving some sort of business goal. So the next logical things that they think about are "serious games" and "advergames"—these subfields of gaming attempt to use games to educate users about a topic or a brand and are even harder to pull off successfully than a normal game. They're games with ulterior motives. If you thought it was hard to create a successful game, think about how hard it is to make one whose whole purpose is to convey educational or advertising content.

Gamification is not about creating games at all. With gamification, your core experience is the centerpiece, and the gamification mechanics go around it. The name itself implies this—you have something that already exists—a website, a loyalty program, or expense-reporting software, and it is being transformed, gamified, with the *addition* of gamification mechanics. And that core experience has to have some intrinsic value of its own. Imagine that you have a website that shows the latest traffic conditions but that only updates once a week. If that's the case, no amount of gamification is going to help you—before you can even think about gamification, you need to refine your core value proposition. Once you have that nailed down, the gamification mechanics can layer on top of it and drive engagement, activity, and loyalty around it.

Games Are Intrinsically Motivating

So clearly gamification isn't building games. But it does have a lot to learn from the world of games because games are so powerful at engaging people. Recall our five intrinsic motivators:

- **Autonomy:** *I control.*
- **Mastery:** *I improve.*

- **Purpose:** *I make a difference.*
- **Progress:** *I achieve.*
- **Social interaction:** *I connect with others.*

You may notice that these motivators are stimulated, to varying degrees, by ordinary games—not just video games, but even ordinary card games, board games such as Monopoly, and others. The enjoyment from playing games comes not just from the joy of winning (after all, what do we really win, anyway?) but also from the path to that win—in which most of these motivators are triggered:

- You have complete *autonomy* to make your own decisions in the course of the game. Should you buy Park Place? Sacrifice your pawn for the greater good? Go all in? Within the framework of the rules, you decide how you want to accomplish your objectives.

- You want to get better at the game—that's the *mastery* motive. When a game loses any ability for you to get better, you quickly grow bored. Little kids love playing tic-tac-toe until they realize that following a simple set of rules will always lead to a tie and that there's no way to get any better, at which point they get bored and move on to the next game. Then, as they grow older and smarter, the same thing happens with Candy Land, Chutes and Ladders, and other games until they finally reach games that require skill, strategy, and meaningful choices. Those games, then, can be played for a lifetime.

- When you're playing a game, you willingly and intentionally set aside the real world and real life and, for the duration of the game, enter what Dutch historian Johan Huizinga referred to as the "magic circle."[1] You are in another world, the game world, and in that world you typically have a single driving *purpose*—to win. And while that win generally won't make any difference in the real world, inside the game world, it is the sole reason for existence.

- Games typically give players a clear sense of their *progress*. If the purpose is to win, then at any point in time, how am I doing toward that goal? Pieces on the chessboard, number of chips in poker, and properties and cash in Monopoly all are clear indicators of progress.

- *Social interaction* is the primary reason many of us play games in the first place. Games give us a magic circle, a virtual world, in which to engage with our friends and family and compete, collaborate, and connect in ways that we don't in real life.

Technology in the gaming world serves only to amplify many of these motivators—you can now play with anyone around the world at any time, track your progress in infinite detail, and engage in experiences that provide even more autonomy ("open-world games") and opportunities for mastery. You also have the opportunity to save statistics about your game play and use those statistics to compete and earn status in a community.

Today, when you play Monopoly with your family and the game is over, it's over. Now suppose that you were capturing statistics about your game and sharing them in an online community. Now you could see how good of a player you were, historically and currently, against your family, others in your city, and even the rest of the world. You could view this against the general population or just against others in your age range or by using any other relevant filter. In addition, if you tracked other statistics besides win/loss, such as properties owned, dollars at the end of the game, and number of hotels built, you could track your progress in those statistics against others as well. The system also could use this data to provide you with goals to work toward, such as "Own Park Place five games in a row."

In this new vision, each game of Monopoly isn't played in isolation—it's been woven into a rich experiential fabric and is part of a larger context. And when each game of Monopoly ends, it throws off a set of statistics into the world that serve to enrich the overall experience and engage the players. This isn't new; every professional sport works exactly the same way. Players, teams, leagues—they're all throwing off statistics that are sliced and diced every which way and that serve to make the experience more interesting and compelling for both the participants and the fans.

Adding the Spark of Gamification Mechanics

It was out of this technological revolution in gaming that most of the key components of gamification were born. Video game designers have known for years how to incentivize and motivate players by leveraging the data their games generate. Whether it's the player's score, enabling players to "level up" at key milestones, providing players with achievements to unlock, or supplying players with a leaderboard of competitors, video games successfully, consistently, and repeatably use data to motivate players to new heights.

Now that same kind of data is available outside video games, from all the systems that we interact with every day. Combine this new big data set with our enhanced understanding of motivation, and we have a powerful mixture to motivate and engage customers, partners, and employees. Much as an electrical spark ignites a fuel mixture in an automobile engine, gamification mechanics become the "spark" that energizes and ignites the mixture of human motivation and big data to provide a compelling user experience, the experience we call *Loyalty 3.0*.

The 10 Key Mechanics of Gamification

We've discussed gamification mechanics in a general sense and offered a few specific examples along the way. Now it's time to go a level deeper and understand the 10 most important individual gamification mechanics and how they might be deployed in a business. These mechanics are inspired from the world of video games but have been proven to work in any context, and they hit on both intrinsic and extrinsic motivations. The descriptions here should give you a good sense of each mechanic, and when we get to the case studies in Part 2, you'll see them all in action.

1. Fast Feedback

Intrinsic motivators: *Mastery, progress*

In a video game, any time you take an action, you receive instant, real-time feedback. You score more points, or you get blown up and you try again. Positive feedback reinforces good behavior, strategy, and tactics, whereas negative feedback enables you to quickly learn and adjust.

Slow feedback loops disconnect the action from the result, making learning difficult and motivation harder, and weakening the power of the feedback. Not to mention that it can be incredibly frustrating—anyone who has ever tried to adjust the temperature of a shower that has a long delay between turning the knob and actually changing the temperature can attest to that.

In online gamification experiences, fast feedback is provided in the form of notifications. These typically appear as "toast" messages, the small windows that slide in from the bottom of the screen that e-mail and instant-messaging clients use to let you know when you have new e-mail or someone is online. In gamification experiences, they're used to let the user know that he's accomplished a goal or hit a milestone, to cross-promote other content and activities, to thank the user, and to suggest a next action for the user to take. This last one is especially important—many of your participants will interact with your experience in very lightweight ways, so your challenge is to pull them down the *participation chain* and motivate them to engage more deeply with you. At a point in time when you're notifying users of success, suggesting a next action is a great way to do that.

2. Transparency

Intrinsic motivators: *Progress, social interaction*
Video games are statistical heaven—players can always see exactly where they stand and where everyone else stands. They can track their progress in real time, see how they're doing now and how they've done historically, and compare themselves with other individuals and the overall community. It's the gaming version of the quantified self.

In online gamification experiences, this encompasses several of the elements you might see—an individual profile page, a list of goals and the user's progress toward them, team profile pages, and both individual and team leaderboard pages. Gamification is motivating people through data, so a big part of the user experience is making that data visible and digestible to users.

3. Goals

Intrinsic motivators: *Purpose, progress, social interaction*
The whole purpose of a game is to have a goal and to strive for

it, such as, "Save the princess," often with secondary goals or subgoals that provide small wins along the way, such as, "Get to the next level" or, "Find all the hidden objects in the room." In the game world, these goals are often called *achievements, challenges,* or *missions.* Without goals to work toward, without milestones to reach, games (and anything else) become grinds—endless repetitive sameness.

Aside from giving participants a purpose, explicitly defined goals also serve to clearly identify to participants what activities are possible in the experience, as well as what behaviors are valued by the program designer. In gamification programs, goals will usually manifest themselves as a simple list that's visible to the participant. Each goal will typically include:

- A description of what needs to be done to accomplish it
- An indication of how much time is left before it expires
- A description of any reward for completing it
- One or more visual indicators showing the user her progress toward the goal
- Indications of others in the community who are working toward or have accomplished this goal

Goals can be of various types, as we'll see in the examples in Part 2, but probably the most important attribute is that they should be personalized (or segmented). Especially in the workplace, "one size fits all" solutions don't work, and the business owner should be able to create goals that are universal and apply to everyone, as well as goals that apply only to specific business units, roles, skill profiles, or even individuals. The participant attributes that are used for personalization can be relatively static things, such as gender and geographic location, or they can be more dynamic, such as, "Has completed training on Product X." This enables participants to see only what's relevant to them, individually, at any point in time.

4. Badges

Intrinsic motivators: *Mastery, progress, purpose, social interaction*
A *badge* is an indicator of a specific accomplishment or conquest of a specific task or skill—think Boy Scout badges or medals in the military. Whether they're physical or virtual, their value is not in the badges themselves but in what they represent in a community. If you weren't in the Boy Scouts and you saw a scout with a badge that had a picture of a cow on it, it wouldn't have any meaning for you. Unless you were a fan of cow badges, if someone gave one to you, you'd probably throw it away.

But if you were a Boy Scout or someone affiliated with the Boy Scouts, you'd know that the badge represented expertise in animal science and that it had taken dedicated time and effort to earn. You'd know how hard it was to get that badge versus all the others, and you'd know that the Boy Scout had visited a farm or raised animals himself to earn it. In that community, badges have a significant meaning, and that's what gives them their ultimate value, both to the individual as a mark of achievement and status, and to the community as a way of identifying engagement, skills, and expertise.

Often badges will be awarded for completing goals, so this gamification mechanic and the previous one are often intimately tied together.

Other interesting ways to use badges include:

- Tapping into people's desires to collect and complete sets (such as baseball cards or any other collectible hobby)
- Enabling users to pick their favorite badges and visibly show them off to their peers

- Creating badges that participants don't know how to earn, so they have to figure it out

- Creating badges that participants don't even know exist, so they are surprised and delighted when they receive them

5. Leveling Up

Intrinsic motivators: *Mastery, progress, purpose, social interaction*
While badges are indicators of specific accomplishments or skills, levels are used as a shorthand way of indicating long-term, sustained achievement and status. Reaching level 70 in World of Warcraft means something to everyone who plays the game, which is that you have dedicated a certain amount of time and energy to the game and achieved a certain amount of skill. Levels also serve to provide players with intermediate goals (small wins) in the long arc of a game.

Levels are one of the gamification mechanics that Loyalty 1.0 programs such as frequent-flyer programs have used for a long time. As you increase your spend, you "level up" to a tier with higher status and better benefits—free checked baggage, early boarding, and better seating, among others.

And as we mentioned earlier in this chapter, employees have been leveling up at work forever—working their way up the corporate ladder in the long arcs of their careers. At work, your level is typically indicated by some combination of your job title, your office, how many people report to you, your responsibilities, your influence, and your salary.

In gamification programs, levels are frequently displayed anywhere that a user's name is shown, as an important, highly visible shorthand indicator of the user's status in the community. Users typically will level up when their point balance reaches certain predefined thresholds or when they accomplish a predefined set of goals. Reaching a level also can act as a key to unlock certain special abilities, goals, badges, content, and rewards.

6. Onboarding

Intrinsic motivators: *Mastery*

Rare is the game that drops you in with no instruction on how to play. And it's never "read the manual" instruction—games have mastered the process of onboarding users, teaching them how to play from within the game itself. Players get live experience at "doing," coached along by the system, until they feel they have sufficient mastery to venture off on their own. The popular social game Farmville is a great example—as simple as it looked, it had concepts such as Experience Points, Farm Coins, Farm Cash, Ribbons, Levels, Planting, Harvesting, and more. If the designers dropped you into the game with a plot of dirt and nothing else, you would have no idea what to do. But they don't—they hold your hand and teach you how to play by actually playing.

In Chapter 1 we discussed how "there's too much to learn" and how that has made educating customers, partners, and employees more and more difficult. Video games have mastered the art of teaching users to play. They take new players through a set of progressively harder skill-building exercises that get the players to learn by doing, and when the players are done, they're ready to go.

It doesn't feel like training, it doesn't look like training, but it is training. And businesses that can train their customers to use their products effectively will drive sales and renewals, businesses that can train their partners how to sell their products better will amplify their revenue, and businesses that can train their employees how to perform more effectively and efficiently will see a direct impact to their top and bottom lines.

Gamification programs often use these onboarding techniques to teach participants complex skills or concepts, and we'll see a great example of this in Chapter 6 when we look at LevelUp for Adobe Photoshop.

7. Competition

Intrinsic motivators: *Mastery, social interaction*

Whether they're competing with friends on an Xbox or people around the world in a virtual world, games foster excellence and achievement through competition. Competition can take many forms, from straightforward leaderboards (high-score tables), to competing for scarce assets, to just wanting to one-up your neighbor.

Focusing specifically on leaderboards, practically every video game ever made has one. It's aspirational, a claim to fame, and your name in lights. It's also a measure of "How am I doing?" against your friends or colleagues and everyone else. Most games have only one because there's only one metric they measure, which is your score. But when you track big data about user activity, you can do a leaderboard on anything—who has shared the most videos, closed the biggest deals, or contributed the best content—and drive competition around it. And all this can be done on an individual level as well as on a team level.

Leaderboards are a double-edged sword, so they should be used thoughtfully. If you have a gamification program with 10,000 participants and a top-100 leaderboard, then 9,900 participants are probably not very motivated by it and in fact may be demotivated. New users who join your program will see the top performers, think "I'll never catch up," and not even bother to engage. There are three ways to implement leaderboards to address this:

- **Use different time frames.** Along with an "all-time" leaderboard, also have a "today" or a "this week" leaderboard. In this way, everyone, regardless of how long they have been participating with your program, always has a chance to get on a leaderboard.

- **Shrink the context.** Instead of showing users a global leaderboard, just show them one with themselves and their friends or their work colleagues. Most people work and play in small enough units that this cuts down the size of the leaderboard to something where the user can always have a place.

- **Show "me."** Rather than always showing the top x, instead, always show current users where they rank, even if they're in 1,000th place, and show them a few people above them and a few people below them. This gives users a sense of where they rank, gives them clear targets for what they need to do to move up rungs of the ladder, and lets them know what they need to do to prevent themselves from moving down rungs. At the end of the day, the most important person to users is themselves.

Finally, competition isn't appropriate in every community. Some are much more focused on collaboration, or community, or mastery, and as such, competition could be out of place. You don't need to use all the gamification mechanics in your program, just the ones that make sense.

8. Collaboration

Intrinsic motivators: *Purpose, social interaction*
From our social-interaction motivator we know that people have an innate need for social connection and as such love to compete and collaborate as part of teams. Teams provide an opportunity to connect and bond with others "like" you (even if the only similar-

ity is that you're on the same team) and work together as a cohesive unit to accomplish goals and compete with other teams. At the same time, the peer pressure of not wanting to let down your peers or be seen as the weakest link can amplify behavior and drive dramatic increases in individual and team performance.

Teams can be as big as your entire community, working together to reach a collective goal, as we'll see in Chapter 5 when we look at Chiquita's "Make Your Way to Rio" promotion. Or they can be smaller and more focused, with multiple teams competing in a "league," as we'll see in Chapter 7 when we take a look at Nitro for Salesforce. And it doesn't take much to make someone feel like part of a team. You can walk into a room and just count people off, "A," "B," "A," and "B," to assign teams, and that's enough for the A's to feel an affinity with each other and a sense of competition with the B's. That affinity is what makes teams so powerful. When people are on teams, they are no longer looking out solely for their own best interests but also for the best interests of the overall team and the other individuals on it. And they're motivated to excel by their desire not to let their colleagues down.

In gamification programs, teams are extremely effective. Teams work together to beat other teams and to collectively accomplish team missions and earn team badges that benefit all the members. In the workplace, teams can be based on obvious structures (e.g., project teams, business units) or not-so-obvious structures (e.g., cross-business unit, cross-geography, random) and used to drive competition, collaboration, networking, and knowledge sharing in an organization.

9. Community

Intrinsic motivators: *Social interaction*
Many of the gamification mechanics described here lose a significant amount of their value without a community—there's

no one to compete with, no one to collaborate with, no one to show off my status to, no one to see my badges, and no sense of life and activity. So community, while not essential, is often a crucial prerequisite for gamification, depending on your context. We're social creatures, so we want to see what others are doing and want them to see what we're doing. The primary mechanism in gamification programs for providing this *ambient awareness* of what everyone is doing is a news feed, much like Facebook's news feed. Gamification systems will automatically add to the news feed any time a user makes a meaningful accomplishment (i.e., completes a mission, earns a badge, or levels up) so that the achievement is socialized to the user's colleagues and to the rest of the community, and they can both notice and respond. The news feed serves multiple purposes:

- To spread the word about participant accomplishments
- To surface and cross-promote people, content, and activities
- To create a sense of life and activity in the experience
- To establish a *social norm* — "these are the accepted behaviors here"
- To let you know what your inner circle of friends or colleagues at work is doing

In gamification programs, typically the experience that's being gamified already has community elements baked in, and the gamification mechanics integrate seamlessly into them. If your experience doesn't currently have community, it's still possible to use gamification, but it may not be as impactful.

10. Points

Intrinsic motivators: *Progress, social interaction*
For participants, points are:

- A number
- That goes up and down
- That indicates how much of something you have
- And that you might be able to spend

For businesses, points are:

- A way of tracking or scoring an attribute of a participant
- A way of rewarding a participant for doing something of value to you
- A way for your participants to reward each other for something
- A way to give your participants spending power

So, in gamification programs, points can be a way of keeping score, such as your number of connections on LinkedIn, in which case their primary function is to convey status. They can be a currency, such as your frequent-flyer miles, which your participants will want to earn and then burn (spend). And they can be the foundation for some of the other gamification mechanics, such as leveling up, as well as a reward for accomplishing goals.

Some other "pointers":

- A gamification program can have multiple types of points so that you can score or reward your users across multiple dimensions. For instance, you might have "sharing" points and "contributing" points, and users would earn the appropriate kind of points depending on the actions they take.
- You can name your points anything, but if the name has a monetary connotation, such as "bucks" or "dollars" in it, then participants will expect to be able to spend them.
- If points are spendable, then separately track each user's

current point balance (what she currently has to spend), as well as her lifetime point balance (the total points she's ever earned—this number only goes up and never goes down). The lifetime point balance typically corresponds to the user's status and level in the community and shouldn't go down when the user buys something.

Figure 4.1 summarizes the 10 primary gamification mechanics.

Fast Feedback	I get immediate feedback or response to actions.
Transparency	I can see where everyone (including me) stands, quickly and easily.
Goals	I have short and long term goals to achieve.
Badges	I can display evidence of my accomplishments.
Leveling Up	I can achieve status within my community.
Onboarding	I can learn in an engaging, compelling way.
Competition	I can see how I'm doing against others.
Collaboration	I can work with others to accomplish goals.
Community	I can see what the community is doing; the community can see me.
Points	I can see tangible, measurable evidence of my accomplishments.

Figure 4.1 THE 10 GAMIFICATION MECHANICS.

Rewards = Meaningful Value

You'll notice that we didn't include rewards in the preceding discussion. Any discussion of rewards will bring us full circle back to the intrinsic versus extrinsic motivation discussion from Chapter 2, where we covered how the line between them is not black and white but a continuum of gray and that there is

Gamification Mechanic Zero: Choice

You may have noticed that the intrinsic motivator of autonomy isn't listed with any of the 10 gamification mechanics. This is because autonomy, in the form of choice, is an integral part of gamification and underlies nearly all the mechanics. Participants in gamification programs have choices: which goals to pursue, how to pursue them, whether to engage in competition or collaboration, how to spend their earned points, and more. And these meaningful choices serve to engage participants while fundamentally affecting the nature and outcomes of their gamification experience.

value in both. With respect to rewards, people often oversimplify and equate extrinsic rewards with cash or cash-value rewards (such as toasters and MP3 players) and intrinsic rewards with anything that has no actual dollar value. Along with that oversimplification goes the belief that extrinsic rewards are universally bad and that intrinsic rewards are universally good. In this framework, most of the elements of gamification would seem to be intrinsic because leveling up, achieving badges, and reaching the top of a leaderboard have no dollar value.

With today's research and experience, we now know better. All those things just mentioned—badges, levels, and so on—are also being motivated from outside as well, so the gamification mechanics are really addressing a mix of intrinsic and extrinsic motivations. This doesn't mean at all that they're bad. I think anyone would be hard pressed to argue that when your boss congratulates you on a job well done, your soccer team votes you captain, and you get a promotion, that those are bad things. I think this gets us to the crux of how we should be thinking about rewards with respect to motivation—rewards need to be something of meaningful value—whether they come from external or internal origins.

The Four Types of Extrinsic Motivation

Even self-determination theory (SDT), which considers intrinsic motivation to be more powerful than extrinsic motivation, acknowledges that not all extrinsic motivation is the same. There is a subtheory of SDT called *organismic integration theory*[2] (OIT) that outlines four different types of extrinsic motivation based on their relative levels of autonomy:

- **External regulation.** Someone is making or incentivizing you to do something. For instance, when my wife tells me to do the dishes, she is externally regulating my behavior.

- **Introjected regulation.** The behavior is related to my ego, self-worth, and self-esteem. Depending on my motivations, going to the gym could be considered introjected.

- **Identified regulation.** This occurs when you consciously value a goal or regulation so that it's accepted as personally important. Religious behaviors often fit into this category.

- **Integrated regulation.** This occurs when you've fully assimilated the regulation or behavior into your being. This is the closest to intrinsic motivation but is still being done for external reasons rather than the joy of the behavior itself. Any kind of behavior, even doing dishes, can become integrated if the context is set appropriately.

In today's business and technology literature, there are several critiques of gamification as a methodology, but they typically boil down to a single point—a belief that the business is deriving value while the participants are getting "meaningless points and badges." And *when gamification is done poorly*, the critics are absolutely correct. Whenever we engage with any system, we all, either explicitly or implicitly, ask, "What's in it for me?" If there's no good answer to this question, we won't engage. The key, then, is to provide something of meaningful value to the end user for participating.

People often take *meaningful value* to mean cash or cash-value rewards. Those certainly have a place, but they're by no means the only kind of reward or necessarily the most motivating. People value *status*, as is clearly indicated by job titles at work and rank in the military. Can you imagine walking up to a senior vice president of something-or-other and telling her that you were leaving every aspect of her job the same—her salary, direct reports, responsibility, and so on but just taking the *senior* out of her job title? Do you think she'd feel a sense of loss? For something that has no tangible value, is just a word on a business card? Absolutely, because that insignificant little word is loaded with meaning and context in her work community.

Recognition and appreciation are simple rewards that can have a profound impact, whether or not they have any monetary value associated with them. There are entire companies such as Globoforce, Achievers, Perks.com, TemboSocial, and salesforce.com's Work.com devoted to providing employee-recognition systems that enable managers and peers to recognize and appreciate each other with both social and monetary rewards.

Early and exclusive access can be very valuable to people. For instance, the Gilt Groupe has a daily-deal site that publishes each day's deal at noon. There is a limited number of each deal, so as a customer, you're in the scrum with everyone else trying to get in on the deal, and maybe you do, maybe you don't. But, if you've spent more than $10,000 with the Gilt Groupe, you "level up" and become a member of "Gilt Noir." Aside from access to special sale events, what's the big benefit? You get in at 11:45 a.m. every day instead of noon, so you have 15 minutes in which you're almost guaranteed to be able to get in on any deal. It costs the Gilt Groupe nothing, but it provides meaningful value to its elite customers.

Now imagine that you're a fan of the queen of pop, the original material girl, Madonna. In fact, you're one of the top 100 fans in her fan club. What if she gave you your choice of reward—either insider access to her tour diary, only available to her top 100 fans, or $100? Which do you think her fans would pick? It's a safe bet that the majority would take the exclusive access—to get "behind the velvet rope" and have access to information that only a select few have, to be special, and to be the hero who shares it with the world. At what point do you think the dollars would win out? $200? $500? $1,000? It's an interesting question and a calculation that happens in each fan's head as he weighs his love for Madonna and desire to be special versus the need for cash.

Then there's *power*—giving people new abilities that they didn't have before. This can be anything from budget authority to spend more at work, to moderation rights in an online community, to the ability to switch your flights at no cost in a frequent-flyer program. Your reward for participating is additional capabilities that enable you to participate in new, previously inaccessible ways.

Finally, there are *prosocial incentives*—enabling participants to give to others. We know that social interaction is one of our key motivators, and a set of experiments performed by Harvard

Business School professor Michael Norton and his collaborators[3] demonstrated just how important it is. In their first experiment, employees who were given money to donate to charities reported a significant increase in their happiness and job satisfaction. And their second experiment showed that when participants were told to spend bonus money on their fellow team members, instead of receiving a standard bonus of money for themselves, their actual job performance increased. The return on investment (ROI) of money spent on incentives? Their experiments with sales teams showed that money given to employees to spend on themselves returned 3 euros to the business for every 10 euros spent—a net loss. Those same 10 euros, when spent on others on the team, returned a stunning 52 euros to the business.

Inherent in the view of the critics mentioned earlier, that there's an unfair value exchange between the business and the user, is a cynical belief that people are dumb and can be taken advantage of indefinitely. I don't believe that this is true—we'll engage with anything for a little while, if only because it's shiny and new, but if we fail to derive meaningful value from our engagement, we'll disconnect and walk away. So it's imperative, when you're thinking about how to apply gamification to your business problems, that you understand what's in it for your end users and what meaningful value you're providing to them.

Questions and Answers

I often get asked why gamification is exploding right now. Why not five years ago? Twenty years ago? The answer ties back to everything that we've been discussing in the preceding chapters. Gamification has been around in primitive forms, Loyalty 1.0, for years but was limited by the data that it was able to work with—purchases. Our shift to living our lives online has accelerated dramatically in the last several years and with that has provided the data set that finally provides gamification with the raw material, the statistics, the big data needed to truly activate and engage participants. Software is eating the world and enabling gamification in the process.

Coincident with that, I often get asked if gamification works only on kids or young adults. While those generations certainly have grown up with the language and metaphors of games and are finely attuned to gamification, the answer is most definitely "No." The techniques that we described in this chapter and the motivators that they leverage are universal, crossing demographics, psychographics, and geographies. I've seen them work in the United States, in Europe, in Latin America, and across Southeast Asia, for kids, young adults, professionals, and senior managers. We are all human, and we can all be motivated by data, as you'll see in Part 2.

As with anything else, gamification can be done well, and it can be done poorly. In any new field that captures the collective imagination like gamification has, you will see companies, driven by the novelty and hype, copying what they see others doing, doing it poorly, and failing. And they do this without any real understanding of why they're doing it, just with a blind faith that if it worked for someone else, it will work for them. I've seen it happen to big and small companies across a range of industries. The leading cause of failure is poor gamification design, which comes from a lack of understanding, experience, and a proven process. My goal with this book is to arm you with the knowledge and tools to make you one of the successes.

A Road Map to Part 2: "Execution"

At this point we depart from the descriptive explanation of the key elements of Loyalty 3.0—motivation, big data, and gamification—to show examples of how all this actually works in

Driving Without a Steering Wheel

I have a friend who was the product manager in charge of a big consumer website, and she would relate to me how every day she'd look at the latest statistics being generated by her web analytics tools. She could see instantly if things were trending up or down, whether people were visiting new areas of the site or not, and how much time people were spending on the site. It was the equivalent of the dashboard in her car, the ability to see exactly what was going on at any point in time. But then what? If she wanted to make a change, it typically involved modifications to the website, which needed to go through the product team and a three- to six-month product cycle. By the time the change went live, it would likely be too late. It was like the doctor hitting her knee and three to six months later she'd kick!

So while her site had a dashboard, it had no steering wheel and no accelerator. She could see exactly what direction it was going in and how fast it was going, but she had no ability to react in real time to the data and insight provided by the dashboard. The business equation has two parts, though—the product and the people who use it. My friend, who didn't have gamification, could focus only on the product and suffered as a result. Gamification, on the other hand, focuses on the people and motivating them to act in a certain way. Because of this, it's easy for a business owner to configure and to modify in real time depending on what is happening with the business.

Have you committed to a sponsor that you'll provide him with a certain amount of exposure in the next three days? Do you have a big event rapidly approaching and need your customers and employees to spread the word?

Are you trying to energize your sales team to hit your number in the last week of the quarter? With the product lens on, you're hosed. But with the gamification (motivating people) lens on, you, the business owner, can make things happen. With gamification, business owners now have a steering wheel and an accelerator and can react instantly to whatever comes their way.

practice. The chapters in Part 2 detail real-world examples of Loyalty 3.0 deployments in an assortment of areas—customer engagement, learning and skill development, and employee motivation. Each case study will discuss the problem the business was trying to solve, the Loyalty 3.0 experience designed to achieve it (which used big data and gamification to motivate participants), and the results and findings.

After looking at these case studies, in Part 3 we'll shift our attention to the strategic and tactical implementation "recipe" for your enterprise, and the future of Loyalty 3.0.

Building Loyalty 3.0

- Gamification is motivating people through data.
- People have been doing it for years, but big data enables it to be automated, to scale, and to motivate behaviors that weren't accessible before.
- Gamification isn't about creating games. It does learn from games, though.
- The 10 gamification mechanics are
  1. Fast feedback
  2. Transparency

3. Goals

4. Badges

5. Leveling up

6. Onboarding

7. Competition

8. Collaboration

9. Community

10. Points

- The key to success is to provide meaningful value to your participants.

- Along with cash or cash-value rewards, other things that people value include:

  o   Status

  o   Recognition and appreciation

  o   Early access

  o   Exclusive access

  o   Power

  o   Prosocial incentives

- This book aims to arm you with everything you need to create a successful Loyalty 3.0 program.

PART
2

EXECUTION

Vision without execution is hallucination.

Thomas A. Edison

CHAPTER 5

Case Studies in Customer Engagement

P art 2 of our journey takes us on a tour of companies that are already implementing Loyalty 3.0 programs and experiencing the benefits. While they may not explicitly refer to them as Loyalty 3.0 programs (given that we're introducing the concept in this book), you'll see the building blocks that we reviewed in Part 1 in all the examples in the next few chapters.

The goal of each case study in this first chapter of Part 2 is to see Loyalty 3.0 in action and to understand how it's enabling businesses to build more durable, useful, and profitable relationships with their *customers*. We use *customer* here to refer to both the typical end-user customers who buy consumer products and watch TV shows in their living rooms as well as business customers who buy products for their companies. In these cases and all that follow in the next two chapters, look for the recurring themes of appeal to basic motivations, applied gamification, and the use of data to chart and change course, as well as create new value.

Characters Welcome at USA Network

Jesse Redniss was psyched. As the senior vice president of digital for USA Network,[1] the number one basic cable network and part of the NBCUniversal family, his mission was to drive market and revenue growth for USA's online content network. And he had an idea. He had recently dipped his toes into the Loyalty 3.0 waters by using big data, motivation, and gamification on USA Network's casual gaming site, Character Arcade, and had seen great results. Now he was convinced that the same techniques could be used to engage fans of the network's TV shows. In particular, the show *Psych*, a detective comedy/drama, had a young, loyal, and rabid audience that was already active online. So the company set out to create a Loyalty 3.0 experience online and on-air to increase engagement with its customer base both when the show aired as well as between shows and between seasons. Enter *Club Psych* (Figure 5.1).

Figure 5.1 THE *CLUB PSYCH* HOMEPAGE.
Source: *Club Psych.*

The core of USA's Loyalty 3.0 strategy is its entertainment content. The foundation, the core intrinsic value that the company is able to build on, consists of several seasons of TV shows combined with thousands of pieces of *Psych* syndicated content (i.e., videos, games, photos, blogs, etc.) online. By enabling its fans to interact with, consume, and share that content, USA receives a rich stream of big data from multiple sources, including web analytics, content-delivery networks, video-on-demand services, social-media monitoring, e-commerce purchase data, and gamification platforms.

That data stream, when captured and analyzed, informs how the company creates content, how it communicates to fans and viewers, and how it modifies its technology and platforms to reach more fans and learn even more about them. As Redniss says, "Big data leads to big insights."[2] And the big-data benefits don't just accrue to the fans, who get a more engaging and meaningful experience, but also to the brands and advertisers that USA works with, who now can target their messaging much more effectively.

As we've discussed, big data is great for learning, but when combined with gamification, it becomes an extremely potent motivational tool. In 2010, USA Network launched *Club Psych*, a digital loyalty and fan engagement program for fans of the *Psych* TV show. *Psych* fans can sign up for *Club Psych* and then when they interact with *Psych* content online — watching videos, sharing to social networks, playing games, taking quizzes, interacting with special promotions, chatting with other fans, and so on — they accomplish goals and earn points. Those points can be redeemed for virtual items that can be used to customize a *Psych*-themed virtual space — a "canvas" where fans can demonstrate their creativity, identity, and status in the community. In addition, points can be spent on limited quantities of *Psych* merchandise—including DVDs, posters, and other branded items—and fans can compete against each other to see who is the biggest *Psych* fan, or "*Psych-o*."

By doing this, the digital team for *Psych* has been able to drive the page views in the *Psych* area of the website from 9 million a month to 16 million, visits per month from 2 to 4.5, and average time on the site from 14 to 22 minutes, as well as generate a 40 percent increase in on-air viewership among the 18 to 34 age demographic.[3] Corresponding advertising inventory and sponsorship opportunities also have increased dramatically. In addition, as fans go into the store to buy *Psych* merchandise that they earned with their points, 47 percent of them buy more stuff with their own cash, generating twice the store's previous average revenue.[4]

Club Psych isn't just a website; the team at USA Network also created a mobile application called *Psych Vision* (Figure 5.2). In the media world today, networks understand that people are often interacting with a phone or tablet while they're watching TV, and they see an opportunity to create a *dual-screen* experience—where the mobile device enhances the experience of what you're watching. They encourage fans to download and interact with the app by integrating it with the live TV experience, both while the show is airing and as it transitions to commercials, and create a multichannel fan experience.

The big data that USA Network collects about online user activity enables the company to implement a powerful motivation strategy using gamification. Gamification amplifies fan engagement with the *Psych* TV show and online *Psych* content, thereby generating even more valuable big data. As we can see, Loyalty 3.0 continually enhances itself over time; it's a virtuous circle.

USA Network has learned many things along the way and adapted its program accordingly. "Gamified sites are like organ-

Figure 5.2 THE *PSYCH VISION* MOBILE APP.
Source: *Club Psych.*

ic beings," says Redniss. "You can't launch and walk away—it is constantly changing and growing."[5] So new missions and other elements are refreshed every day during the show's season and every few days in the off-season. The company also learned to publicize new content in *Club Psych* by posting updates on social networks every time a new mission is released.

While *Club Psych* is a long-term strategy and platform for maintaining sustained, ongoing engagement, USA Network also learned that it could launch successful short-term campaigns. One example of this was Campus Wars, where college students and alumni could collaboratively work together as a college team to recruit more *Psych-os*, gain points, and compete for the ultimate prize of having their school logo included in an episode of the TV show. More than 11,000 colleges created teams, and the winning team from Brigham Young University (BYU) had 1,500 members.[6] *Psych* fans were recruiting their friends, families, and peers with personal endorsements, the most powerful form of recommendation, and the company didn't have to shell out a huge monetary incentive to make it happen, just recognition and status for the winning team.

USA Network continues to push the boundaries of traditional on-air series, most recently with a transmedia campaign called Hashtag Killer. Over the course of seven weeks, fans interacted with *Psych's* stars, Shawn and Gus, across multiple digital platforms to help them crack the case of the Hashtag Killer. Big data was being collected across all these platforms, and gamification was a key component in motivating participants to engage. The results were notable: 95 million page views from 300,000 unique users, 288,000 "shares" on Facebook leading to 38 million exposures of the *Psych* brand to users' friends and families, over 14 million minutes spent participating in the Hashtag Killer program,[7] and a nomination for an Emmy for outstanding creative achievement in interactive media.[8] Through these various short- and long-term efforts, USA is engendering true loyalty in its audience base. *Psych* fans aren't just passive viewers and consumers of content, they are active participants in the *Psych* world, with choices about how they engage, goals that give them purpose, a community of people to compete and collaborate with, and meaningful rewards.

Looking forward, USA plans for its Loyalty 3.0 program to provide the data foundation for what it calls a "responsive publishing" platform. In the same way that *responsive design* is now being used by web developers to create content that adjusts itself dynamically to the user's viewing device, whether it's a mobile phone, tablet, or desktop PC, "responsive publishing" will leverage big data and what USA now knows about its viewers to always get the right content to the right user at the right time on the right device.

USA Network and its efforts around *Club Psych* are a great example of a media company living in a cross-platform world that is using big data and gamification to drive engagement and loyalty with its fans and in the end drive meaningful business results. According to Redniss, "*Club Psych* has become the backbone of how we're modeling our future community engagement strategies." [9]

- **Concept.** A digital loyalty program designed to engage the fans of a TV show and reward them for their active participation

- **Business goals.** More engagement, which leads to more ad impressions (online and on-air), sponsorship opportunities, viral audience growth, and merchandise sales

- **Gamification mechanics.** Fast feedback, transparency, goals, competition, collaboration, points

- **Big data.** User activity, e-commerce, video-on-demand, content-delivery networks, social-media monitoring, web analytics

- **Results.** A dramatic increase in online engagement,

increase in page views, increase in visits per month, increase in time on the site, increase in viewership of the TV show, increase in merchandise sales

Going Gaga for MTV MegaFan

What would you do to help your favorite musical artist win an award from MTV? In 2011 and 2012, in the months leading up to the MTV European Music Awards (EMAs), MTV ran a program called MegaFan on its desktop and mobile websites across multiple countries and languages.[10] Fans earned points on the site for watching past EMA performances, viewing "photo flipbooks" of past shows, reading articles, and completing weekly challenges. Fans didn't just earn these points for themselves; they also joined the team of their favorite artist and earned points for that team in a "Biggest Fans" competition. According to MTV, Lady Gaga repeatedly claimed that her 2011 Biggest Fans award meant the most to her of all the awards she received because it came directly from her "monsters"—that is, her fans.[11]

According to Gary Ellis, vice president of international digital media at Viacom International Media Networks, "It was all about increasing engagement with the content. Time spent increased, the overall engagement increased, and whether or not the activity happened on a PC, a smart phone or a tablet, everything connected to all the social networks and with each other."[12]

Make Your Way to Rio with Chiquita Brands

Marketing has always been driven by equal parts creativity and data. But despite the newfound ability to capture more and more data about how consumers are engaging with your brand, the data alone doesn't help you to answer the fundamental questions: How do you create marketing content that engages with, instead of talks at, consumers? Make people want to share your marketing message? Motivate consumers to learn about your brand voluntarily?

Loyalty 3.0 and gamification provide the answers. In 2011 Chiquita Brands,[13] a consumer food products supplier best known for bananas but also for many other fresh and processed fruit and vegetable products, partnered with Twentieth Century Fox to promote a new animated movie, *Rio*, along with a variety of Chiquita products. The company used gamification to drive consumer engagement and participation.

Working with marketing agency Empower MediaMarketing, Chiquita built the *Make Your Way to Rio* website (Figure 5.3), "an engaging online playground for our Chiquita Banana consumer where the whole family could share in the fun of

Figure 5.3 THE *MAKE YOUR WAY TO RIO* HOMEPAGE.
Source: *Chiquita.*

Chiquita-branded products, the film *Rio*, and win great prizes including tasty Chiquita Bananas and other nutritious products," according to Scott Facheux, North America consumer marketing manager at Chiquita Brands. From its data, Chiquita knew that moms were spending more and more time online with their kids, so the company crafted the website specifically for moms and kids to experience together.

Consumers who signed onto the site received a virtual passport (Figure 5.4) which they could fill up with banana sticker "badges" by accomplishing goals throughout the site, including watching movie clips, sharing recipes, playing games, and reviewing product information.

Figure 5.4 THE BANANA STICKER PASSPORT.
Source: *Chiquita.*

A live news feed displayed throughout the site showed a constantly scrolling ticker of badges earned, which served multiple purposes. First, it gave each participant her "15 seconds of fame" because her name was entered into the news feed each time she accomplished a goal. Second, it created a sense of life and activity on the site and gave the participants the sense that they weren't there alone. And finally, it served as a way of establishing social norms for the site—"If other people are doing behavior *x*, then I should be too," and you know that it's possible because you've seen others do it. Remember our *community* gamification mechanic? The news feed implements it perfectly.

So why would consumers care about their banana sticker badges? What meaningful value were consumers receiving for engaging? The badges looked cool and gave users goals to accomplish, and earning them established consumers as part of a community, but the real meaningful value came in making the badges a key component in the *Make Your Way to Rio* Sweepstakes.

When looked at through a Loyalty 3.0 lens, most sweepstakes have two fundamental flaws:

1. Entering takes seconds, doesn't require or generate any engagement or loyalty, and doesn't generate any return visits.

2. There's no incentive to tell anyone else about the sweepstakes because that just reduces your chances of winning.

To address these flaws, the site designers made the sweepstakes progressive and incorporated the badges earned by the community. "The Chiquita community themselves have the power to unlock varying levels of prizes, increasing in value, by earning badges through differing interactions with the site," said Faucheux. "This incentivizes consumers to play more often and also interact more frequently with our brands online."

Do you see the number in the upper left-hand corner of Figure 5.4? That's the total number of badges earned collectively by the community. Now jump back to Figure 5.3, the main page, and take a look at the big progress bar on the bottom. Every time the community collectively earns another 25,000 badges, a new set of prizes is unlocked. At 25,000 badges, the entire community earns a coupon for a Chiquita product, and the fourth-place prizes are unlocked for someone to win. The same happens at 50,000 and at 75,000 badges. And the grand prize of a family trip to Rio de Janeiro? Unlocked and available to win only when the community has earned 100,000 badges.

Your participation in this sweepstakes now requires your engagement and participation; it's not a "one and done" scenario. It also encourages you to tell others about the site because only with a critical mass of active users will the prizes be unlocked, and the more people who participate, the faster the prizes will unlock. Working alone, nobody benefits; working together as a team, everyone does. Remember the *collaboration* gamification mechanic? That's in full force here.

During the course of this marketing campaign, the *Make Your Way to Rio* website received over 1 million page views and had 800,000 unique site visits and 5.6 million word-of-mouth impressions.[14] By leveraging the user-activity data generated by these consumers, Chiquita now knows the types of content that they prefer, when and how they prefer to interact, and which of the company's products have marketing messages that resonate the strongest. In addition, because engaging with the site required users to register, Chiquita has increased the size of its marketing database—information that typically had been hard for Chiquita to collect (you don't typically register when you buy bananas). The next time the company launches a marketing campaign, it won't be starting from zero in trying to attract new users. The company has a warm audience that is already interested in Chiquita that it can reach out to.

While USA Network has the benefit of popular TV shows to drive true loyalty around, Chiquita's core products (bananas) are much less engaging and much more commoditized. This makes it even more important for Chiquita to build a relationship with its customers that transcends its products. By using Loyalty 3.0 techniques, Chiquita was able to create a marketing campaign that engaged consumers with its content, encouraged them to share, and made consumers feel like part of a bigger team that could accomplish big goals together.

- **Concept.** A marketing campaign designed to engage customers of a consumer packaged goods brand and build a deeper relationship with them
- **Business goals.** Increase brand awareness, favorability, and interest in Chiquita products
- **Gamification mechanics.** Fast feedback, transparency, goals, badges, collaboration, community, points
- **Big data.** User activity, content preferences, product preferences, social-media sharing
- **Results.** Increase in engagement, page views, visits, and additional customers and customer data in the marketing database

Innovating in Marketing with Loyalty 3.0

In the age of distraction, it's imperative that your marketing campaign break through the noise, engage consumers, and motivate them to want to participate. One-way broadcast just doesn't cut it anymore—consumers expect to interact. And the data that consumers generate as they're interacting gives you real-time insight into what they're thinking and the opportunity to optimize on the fly. Major brands such as Hewlett-Packard (HP), Right Guard, Wendy's, and Univer-

sal Studios[15] have realized this and have upgraded their marketing campaigns with Loyalty 3.0 principles. It's not hard
to see how these campaigns go beyond the traditional "talk
at you" approach—they seek engagement, not just interest.
Here's a sample of some of the results that they've seen:

HP Campus Karma. A campaign targeted at increasing the
computer maker's Facebook fan base and sparking community, dialogue, and word of mouth.[16]

- Facebook fans grew 26-fold in three months.
- Fan engagement increased 118 percent.
- Page views increased 33 percent.

Wendy's Fry-For-All. A campaign to rally the Wendy's fan
base around the launch of Wendy's new sea-salt fries, with
the goal of earning 40,000 "likes" on Facebook during an
eight-week campaign.[17]

- Goal was achieved in the first 72 hours.
- Word-of-mouth spread virally on blogs and forums.
- Finished with over 150,000 new fans.

Right Guard Total D MVP. A campaign targeted at driving awareness, relevance, and trial for a new Right Guard
product, TD5.[18]

- There were 375,000 incremental trials of TD5.
- Return on investment was greater than 300 percent.
- Impact on pre/post key-brand measures among Total D
  MVP participants:
  - Brand for me: +366 percent

o   Recently tried for first time: +925 percent
o   Definitely would buy in the next three months: 550 percent
o   Recommended TD5 to friend: +1,300 percent

Insider Rewards at Warner Bros.

Movie studios have always had a problem building a direct relationship with consumers. Consumers watch movies at theaters and buy movies at physical and online retailers—so at no point are they ever interacting directly with the movie studio—the actual creator of the product. In 2009, Warner Bros. launched a loyalty program, called Insider Rewards, that connected the company directly with its consumers and that rewarded consumers for watching and buying the studio's products.[19] The company had the key insight (and foresight) that loyalty was no longer just a function of how many dollars a consumer spent with the company but also a function of the consumer's attention and engagement online. Loyalty 3.0 provided the perfect framework for the company to build on.

Attention is a new currency, and because it's so scarce (remember, we are living in the age of distraction), it's valuable. Most traditional loyalty programs don't place any value on your attention, only on the dollars you spend with them, so they're not generating true loyalty. Instead, they're stuck in the old world of Loyalty 1.0 that we described in Chapter 1. In the case of Warner Bros., the company understood that visiting its movie sites, watching trailers, sharing to the social networks, sharing opinions, and providing data about likes and dislikes had a real, meaningful value to the business and that the company should be motivating and rewarding its customers for doing so.

The Warner Bros. Insider Rewards loyalty program had two currencies you could earn. *Points* were earned for purchases—buying DVDs, movie tickets, digital downloads, and so on. Points could be redeemed for more of the same kinds of dollar-value items—pretty traditional Loyalty 1.0 stuff. But the company also added a second currency called *Credits*, which were earned for visiting movie sites, playing games, sharing to social networks, and so on. Credits could be redeemed for Warner Bros. digital content—wallpapers, ringtones, MP3s, and videos—content that fans wanted that could be fulfilled instantly and at little to no incremental cost. It's yet another virtuous circle—consumers engaged with Warner Bros. content in order to earn the right to access even more content.

Note that the separation of Points and Credits here is very smart. Points are a "dollars in, dollars out" system, and Credits are an "activity in, digital content out" system. The most expensive thing you can do in a situation such as this is create an "activity in, dollars out" system, where you're effectively paying users for their activity, and you've unwittingly created a black hole for dollars where your users will give you unlimited amounts of their attention, and you will be on the hook for unlimited amounts of dollars! That's not to say that this is always a bad idea, just that you need to be aware of what you're doing and put appropriate controls in place. "Activity in, dollars out" has worked very well for USA Network's *Club Psych*, but that's because the company has limited a quantity of dollar-value items that can be purchased with points, and it uses sponsors to cover the costs of those items, so there's no money coming out of the company's pockets.

By implementing a Loyalty 3.0 program combining transactional purchase data with online activity data, Warner Bros. was able to realize a number of benefits straight out of the Loyalty 3.0 playbook:

1. The company had the ability to track and reward online activity and engagement.

2. The company was able to measure which activities and content on its sites were the most compelling and the most viral.

3. The company was able to segment its audience based on activity; for instance, "Get me a list of all the consumers who watched the trailer for *The Watchmen* in the last two weeks so that I can send them a special offer on the DVD."

4. The company had a currency that it could use to funnel people between its various properties. Fans of *Harry Potter* now could be incentivized, with Credits, to visit the *Where the Wild Things Are* site and watch the movie trailer.

5. The company had a direct relationship with a group of people that was a "warm" audience that the company could market to anytime a new movie or home video release came out.

6. The company had currencies that it could trade with consumers in exchange for more data. "Tell us your favorite movie genre and earn 100 Credits." I know that whenever a website asks me for more than the basic information I need to register, my immediate reaction is always, "No way!" because usually the business is getting something, and I'm getting nothing. Once the business has a currency that I care about, it can offer me something of value for volunteering my data, and it becomes a fair transaction.

7. The company had more customer data than ever before. It was able to correlate offline purchase data with online activity data and explicit data entered by customers to create a 360-degree view of its customers.

How much better could you market to people if you knew what DVDs they had purchased, what movies they had seen in the theater, what movie sites they had visited, what trailers they had shared to the social networks, and what star rating they had applied to each of your films? The amount of useful information was staggering and gave Warner Bros. the ability to market with much more relevancy and specificity than ever before.

- **Concept.** A loyalty program that rewarded attention and activity, as well as purchases
- **Business goals.** Get customers to buy more. Drive brand engagement and affinity with Warner Bros. as well as the individual movie properties. Increase viral sharing and audience growth. Develop deeper customer intimacy and knowledge.
- **Gamification mechanics.** Fast feedback, transparency, leveling up, points
- **Big data.** User activity, purchase data, content preference, social-media sharing
- **Results.** More customer data and intimacy, activated audience, better segmentation, content optimization

Checking in with Foursquare

Remember the old days, before cell phones, when you'd try to arrange to do something with a group of friends? If someone was running late or lost or some members of the group decided that they wanted to go somewhere else, there was no way to connect and coordinate. Everything had to be planned in advance and then executed according to plan, or people were left behind. Cell phones changed all that, enabling "just-in-time" scheduling. But even then, calling or texting an entire group of friends to update or alter plans was time-consuming at best and infeasible at worst, particularly in big cities where friends might migrate frequently from location to location looking for the "hot spot" and where the group might grow and shrink as the night progressed.

To solve this coordination issue, in 2009 Dennis Crowley and Naveen Selvadurai launched Foursquare, a mobile application that enables users to "check in" to a physical location by pressing a button on their GPS-enabled smart phone. By checking in, users broadcast to their friends where they are and what they're doing in real time. This makes it easy for users to see where all their friends are and what they're doing at any point in time, and it enables groups of friends to coordinate efficiently in real time and at scale.

From its inception, Foursquare has included several gamification elements to encourage users to go out, explore new places, and check in, including:

- Points, which have no redeemable value
- Badges, which can be earned by checking into various venues
- Mayorship, which can be earned by checking into a venue on more days than anyone else in a 60-day rolling time window

As it has scaled to a larger audience, the Foursquare team has added more functionality geared toward interacting with the physical environment, including creating and consuming tips about places to visit, a view of places that are hot and trending, and the ability to create a to-do list of places the user wants to visit. The company also has increased its focus on connecting customers to local businesses, enabling business owners to attract customers, share updates, offer specials, and broadcast events via Foursquare.

Foursquare also uses its big data to create new value-added services. The company's data sources include nearly 3 billion check-ins from over 25 million people worldwide, the tips that users are creating, likes and dislikes that their users are tagging locations with, how popular locations are with their users, how loyal a venue's customers are, and more. By processing and analyzing this data Foursquare is able to:

- Recommend places to you based on your activity and that of your friends and people like you

- Intelligently filter search results based on what it knows about you

- Provide ratings for locations based on a mix of data that users explicitly enter (likes, dislikes, tips) as well as data that users implicitly generate (checking-in), providing a more robust rating system than a typical five-star rating system

- Provide local business owners with detailed analytics about their customers, enabling them to see who is checking in, segmented by time and demographics such as age and gender, and how users are sharing their check-ins to Facebook, Twitter, and other social networks

Foursquare is a great Loyalty 3.0 example, both for its successes and for its failures. In order to generate revenue and create a sustainable business, Foursquare needs to encourage users to initially adopt Foursquare and then to keep entering and generating data about their interactions with the physical world. By integrating gamification into its product from its inception, Foursquare has been able to very effectively onboard new users into the Foursquare experience, engaging them in an experience where they're earning status, unlocking badges, and competing for "mayorships" in a community of friends and peers.

As we discussed in Chapter 4, gamification can provide a short-term lift on almost anything because anything shiny and new will attract attention for at least a little while. But in order to sustain long-term engagement and utilization, the core experience that is being gamified needs to provide value on its own that gamification can then amplify. Foursquare's challenge has been that many of its users haven't yet figured out what that value is. Without some intrinsic value to the service, users who are onboarded and engaged by the gamification eventually will "churn out" and not come back. So, while Foursquare has been very successful at onboarding users, it has been a challenge to retain them.

This is a great lesson for anyone considering using Loyalty 3.0 and gamification—focus on your core product or service first, and make sure that it has some sustainable, intrinsic core value to your users. Only then should you start thinking about how you can drive motivation and engagement around it. Once you have a great product and you're engaging and motivating your users around it, then start using the data they're generating to create even more business value.

- **Concept.** A mobile application that encourages exploration and experimentation
- **Business goals.** Attract users, collect explicit user-entered data and implicit user-generated data
- **Gamification mechanics.** Fast feedback, transparency, goals, badges, competition, community, points
- **Big data.** Check-ins, tips, likes/dislikes, visit frequency, likelihood to return, to-do lists
- **Results.** Over 25 million users worldwide, who have made close to 3 billion check-ins

Contributor Reputation with SAP
Community Network

In 2003, business software giant SAP AG launched the SAP
Developer Network,[20] an online community for its customers, where they could get technical assistance, best practices,
education, and more on SAP products. Since then, the community has grown to over 2 million members from around the
world, broadened its audience to anyone interacting with SAP
products (including developers, consultants, analysts, process
experts, thought leaders, systems integrators, and SAP employees), and changed its name to *SAP Community Network* (SCN).
With millions of members, thousands of discussions every day,
and hundreds of thousands of pieces of informational content,
SAP recognized that SCN provided the perfect stream of big
data to build into a Loyalty 3.0 program.

Of the many ways that the Internet has revolutionized
business, the new channels for business-to-customer interaction have had some of the greatest impact. Before the Internet, methods to get customer feedback, identify power users,
involve customers in product design, and enable customers
to help themselves and each other were primitive and hard
to scale. Technology companies such as SAP were among the
first to realize that they could change the customer-interaction
paradigm and that their businesses could benefit tremendously
as a result.

For SAP's customers, SCN provides:

• Content, including blogs, technical documentation, busi-
ness-process best practices, and special features

• Collaboration opportunities via forums and wikis, where
members can engage with each other

- Downloads and tools of SAP software, templates, plug-ins, tools, and code snippets

- Skill development through online tutorials, videos, demos, and premium training

- A community-driven online solutions marketplace

For customers, SCN enables a greater return on their SAP investment by being able to leverage and build on existing experiences, solutions, and best practices from other customers, partners, experts, and SAP employees. To get these benefits, it's important for customers to have access to the highest-quality content and people in the network to engage with. To that end, SAP created the Contributor Reputation Program, a program designed to keep SCN members engaged and actively providing quality content, to gather their feedback on what was valuable to them, and to thank them by helping to grow their reputation as SAP professionals.

The SCN Contributor Reputation Program uses an assortment of motivators:

- SCN members earn points for their contributions (including authoring documents, code samples, videos, blogs, etc.).

- They earn additional points when community members recognize the value of their contributions by liking, rating, or sharing their content.

- Top participants in each topic area are showcased on the relevant topic pages on a leaderboard.

- Active contributors (based on their activity in a 12-month rolling window) level up from bronze to silver to gold to the platinum level.

- Any time a member reaches a new level, he receives a special "Acknowledgement of Achievement" from SAP via e-mail.

- Once a year, the top three contributors in each of 50 different topics are recognized as "Topic Leaders" at SAP's annual TechEd conferences.

- The top community influencers are nominated by their peers to become SAP Mentors (shown at work in Figure 5.5) based on their passion for the community, their contributions, and their helpfulness.

Figure 5.5 SAP MENTORS AT WORK.
Source: SAP, *Aslan Noghre-kar.*

Through the Contributor Reputation Program, SAP has been able not only to motivate the contribution of high-quality content, but also to create a system where members can build a reputation with direct career impact. Businesses looking for experts, companies looking to hire employees, and SAP event planners looking for people to be involved in corporate events are all looking at SCN member reputations and contributions to decide whom they should engage with.

According to Mark Yolton, senior vice president of digital, social, and communities at SAP, "Top contributors are the backbone of our community. Not only do they provide valuable content, but they inspire others to participate and set the tone for a vibrant exchange of ideas and opinions. The Contributor Reputation Program further encourages and rewards participation to benefit both the individual and the broader SCN family."

Aside from using member activity data to power the Contributor Reputation Program, SAP is also able to extract intelligence from that activity data as well as the thousands of conversations occurring on SCN. This intelligence is used to equip product and marketing teams with insight into hot topics, burning issues, and new opportunities. The insights mined from this data can lead to higher-quality solutions and innovations that better meet SAP customers' needs and therefore have greater market success and impact.

Beyond the community network, SAP also uses Loyalty 3.0 tools to enhance innovation. The platform to capture this kind of insight and innovation is called *Idea Place*—a crowd-based, collaborative way for SAP to co-innovate with its customers, partners, and the greater SAP ecosystem. On Idea Place, members can submit ideas to improve an SAP solution or service, connect with others to refine their ideas, and finally vote to prioritize the best ideas. The "finalists" are then reviewed by a team from SAP that uses the community's prioritization and the strategic fit with SAP's product road map to determine which ideas will have the strongest impact and will be developed.

"It took a heck of a lot of work over nine years to get that network to where we are today. But I do think that it's a strategic advantage for us," says Yolton. "I wouldn't measure it in the size of the community of 2 million people. When I really get down to it, I would really measure it in sort of a loyalty index, or an engagement index. Because I look at other companies in our industry, some competitors and some partners and friends, and they have communities, too, that are either larger or smaller. But I look at the level of engagement in our community, and it's just extraordinary . . . and fulfilling because it's so personally engaging."[21]

By leveraging the big data generated by its customer community, SAP has been able to create a valuable resource for its customers while at the same time giving them a forum to share their feedback and insights with SAP and enabling them to establish a meaningful reputation in the SAP community.

- **Concept.** A community site that enables customers of a software company to communicate with the company and with each other, as well as to develop their reputations as professionals

- **Business goals.** Reduce support costs, share knowledge and best practices, create product champions, get customer insights, co-innovate

- **Gamification mechanics.** Fast feedback, transparency, goals, badges, leveling up, competition, collaboration, community, points

- **Big data.** User activity, quality measures, conversation mining, idea generation

- **Results.** SCN has a world class Net Promoter Score (NPS) of 46 percent. Since its inception, over 400,000 members have contributed their knowledge and experience. Some 361 product ideas have been implemented from Idea Place.

More Loyalty 3.0 Communities

Savoring the First Taste with Kraft Canada

Technology companies aren't the only ones that can benefit from customer communities. Kraft Canada created the First Taste program to enable its fans to interact with each other while also enjoying exclusive, early access to new recipes, products, flavors, and ideas from Kraft experts.

First Taste members (called *FirstTasters*) are rewarded with redeemable points for trying and rating products, making and bookmarking recipes, writing and commenting on blogs, and sharing with other members, friends, and family on social networks and by e-mail. Points can be redeemed for product coupons, kitchen gear, and designs to customize members' personal First Taste kitchen pages. Along with points, FirstTasters also can earn badges by achieving certain goals, and they can compete with other members to see who can accomplish the most.

With First Taste, Kraft Canada is engaging fans in a community where it can solicit their real-time opinions on both existing products and new concepts to help the company better serve its customers and ensure successful products.

Straight to the Top Line with Eloqua Topliners

Marketing automation company Eloqua (recently acquired by enterprise software giant Oracle) offers another example of Loyalty 3.0 principles within a business-to-business (B2B) community to build engagement around a software product.[22] Eloqua runs the Jive Software–powered Topliners community for people in marketing and sales who are interested in marketing automation and revenue performance management. (Topliners is a reference to "top-line revenue" on an income statement.) In

July 2012, the company added gamification to its community, including points that could be earned for interaction and quality contribution, levels that users could strive for, and badges to indicate goals and milestones. The impact was immediate, as you can see in Figure 5.6.

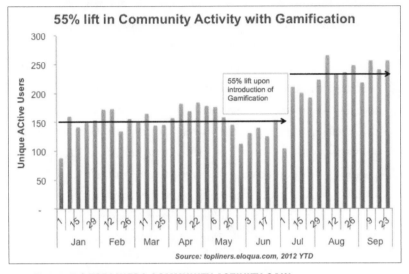

Figure 5.6 TOPLINERS COMMUNITY ACTIVITY GAIN WITH GAMIFICATION.
Source: Eloqua.com, ©2012.

According to Heather Foeh, director of customer culture at Eloqua, "In the chart you'll see that from January through July 2012 we had a fairly steady number of active users per week on the site, despite the fact that our number of registered users grows by about 30 percent per month. You'll even notice the summer lull that started in June and continued through mid-July that we experience each year. But check out the 55 percent spike in average active users in mid-July: that was the week that we launched the gamification changes on our community. Since then we've seen continued excellent growth in activity and engagement on our site."

Foeh continues, "I've been blown away by how much people have gotten into it. We have people following and helping others more, engaged in day-to-day conversation, posting status updates to celebrate the progress they're making, and noting how points and badges fuel their Topliners addiction. All this has resulted in a more engaged, loyal, and active user community—and we're seeing benefits in everything from reduced support calls to increased subscription renewals."

Since gamifying Topliners in July 2012, Eloqua has realized a return on investment (ROI) in several areas:

- **Engagement soars.** Member participation has increased so much that Eloqua had to add a new top level called "Rock Star" because so many people reached the previous top level, "Ninja."

- **Support agents reduced field calls by 40 percent.** An active and responsive community helps drive down support costs. Eloqua's support organization estimates that for every 100 conversations started in the Topliners Do It section, they save 40 phone calls into the company's support line. Because the Do It section sees an average of 300 new conversations every month, that translates to approximately 120 support calls saved monthly.

- **Gamification helps drive renewal.** Eloqua sees gamification as a key contributor to increasing subscription renewals. Topliners members have a much higher renewal rate; 82 percent of renewing customers have at least one user on Topliners, while Topliners participation is far lower among nonrenewing customers. And in surveys, customers cite their ability to belong to Topliners as a major reason for renewing their Eloqua subscription.

- **Eloqua's engaged community is a factor in software sales.** Sales prospects regularly cite Topliners as a reason for choosing Eloqua; they find it reassuring that such an active community is available to them as a resource.

- **Topliners is easier to administer.** As Topliners has become more engaged, it has also become more self-moderating and mutually helpful, which means community managers can spend less time monitoring and moderating discussions and answering questions.

- **Gamification has created a more cohesive community.** Topliners have become so engaged online that they arrange real-world meet-ups at industry events.[23]

By integrating elements of reputation and gamification into its customer community, Eloqua has been able to drive a sustained increase in activity and engagement and, in doing so, create more value for all parties.

Flashes of Brilliance at Redding.com

Redding.com is the website for the *Redding Record Searchlight*, a local northern California newspaper and part of the E. W. Scripps Company. According to Silas Lyons, the paper's editor, "Like many newspapers, we struggle with the comment area becoming a complete cesspool with some flashes of brilliance, but it is a point of high engagement with the users."[24]

Staff members were spending an inordinate amount of time moderating comments on the site, to the detriment of their other duties. In an attempt to increase the signal-to-noise ratio on the site, Redding.com implemented a reputation system where commenters can have their comments marked as "insightful" by other members. As you earn more "insightful" votes, you level up in the community, and your insightfulness level is prominently displayed next to your name.

As Lyons explained to readers when the program first launched, "We think this will allow Redding.com readers to judge for themselves which comments are worth reading and which commenters are worth their attention. We also suspect it will provide some motivation to put just a bit more thought into comments before they're posted."[25] After three months, "we saw a 10 percent increase in comment volume, and the time spent on site increased by about 25 percent per session,"[26] said Lyons. He also noted that despite an overall increase in the number of comments, the number that had to be removed fell noticeably.

By using Loyalty 3.0 principles to build reputation into their news site, the editors at Redding.com have been able to encourage higher quality comments from their readers, as well as an increase in overall quality.

Extending Products Through Community: SolarWinds' Thwack[27]

When customer-support calls can cost anywhere from $5 to $20 and up, how do you empower your customers to help each other as well as themselves? How do you get your customers to give you really good, shareable feedback? How do you get them to give you crowdsourced ideas for further enhancements and applications of your products?

SolarWinds, a software company that develops and markets network applications and virtualization and storage management software, created the Jive Software–powered customer community *thwack* to reduce call-center costs, provide more robust and real-time support, and foster the development and validation of product enhancements. By integrating elements of reputation and gamification, including goals around contributing quality support content, status for quality contributions, and a community of people to compete against, SolarWinds has seen a large boost in support quality and a meaningful reduction in support cost.

Thwack is especially interesting, however, because it goes beyond traditional support into other areas that can help the community. SolarWinds encourages members to submit "product extensions." These are user-defined templates, reports, scripts, and other overlays, analogous to macros for spreadsheets or other commonly used software. Community members are rewarded with points for submitting these extensions on the Content Exchange, with rewards increasing as the adoption of the extension increases. So members are directly enhancing SolarWinds' products, and the better their enhancement, the more rewards and reputation they earn.

Community members are also incentivized to do beta and "release candidate" testing of new software products (Figure 5.7), and to submit ideas for future enhancements through an Ideation page, another good example of crowdsourcing product features and enhancements.

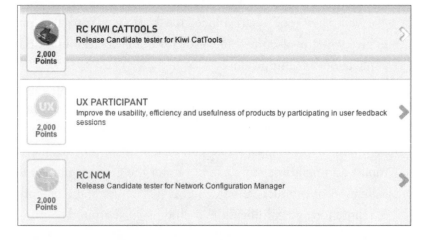

Figure 5.7 SOME THWACK MISSIONS.
Source: *SolarWinds Worldwide, LLC.*

According to Michael Torok, SolarWinds' director of community, "Gamification of [the thwack site] needed to be subtle yet engaging. We needed to avoid the look of a video game in our IT community while still providing the intrinsic rewards and drivers." Thwack serves to involve and engage current and potential users and turn them into brand advocates and "experts" for the company's products—at little to no cost to the company and with an engaging experience for members.

Wrapping It Up

In this chapter we've seen how a variety of companies are using Loyalty 3.0 principles to engage and motivate customers across media, marketing, loyalty, and community. By combining big data with motivation, gamification, and reputation, these companies are able to drive meaningful business results and a competitive advantage in their markets. Next up: Using Loyalty 3.0 to motivate skill development and learning.

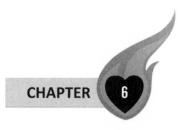

CHAPTER 6

Case Studies in Skills and Learning

W hen was the last time you had to learn something new? It typically starts out hard, but then, as you master the necessary skills and develop confidence in your abilities, you "level up" and are ready for the next tier of difficulty.

What about changing a habit? That's even more challenging because you're trying to force a new pattern to take the place of an old pattern, such as getting up and going to the gym instead of sleeping in or eating carrots instead of cupcakes. And the old patterns (i.e., sleep and cupcakes) often provide more immediate, tangible gratification than the new patterns (i.e., gym and carrots), making the transition difficult.

In this chapter we're going to see how innovative companies are using Loyalty 3.0 principles to motivate people to learn new skills, to master new tools, to change their behavior and form new habits, and to "level up" in their lives.

Getting Fit with Zamzee

In 2001, Pam Omidyar, a scientist, game enthusiast, and wife of eBay founder and chairman Pierre Omidyar, established

HopeLab as a nonprofit entity with the mission to use the power and appeal of technology to improve the health of kids. In 2006, the organization set its sights on sedentary behavior among kids, a major factor in the rise of childhood obesity. With support from the Robert Wood Johnson Foundation, HopeLab developed Zamzee,[1] a Loyalty 3.0 product designed to motivate kids to be more physically active. Research evaluating the impact of early Zamzee prototypes proved so successful that HopeLab decided to launch Zamzee as a stand-alone business in 2010 in order to scale the impact of the Zamzee product and improve the health of kids and families across the United States.

The Zamzee product has two main components. The first is a wearable activity meter that looks very much like a USB flash drive. The meter uses multidirectional motion sensors (accelerometers), similar to those found in smart phones, to capture the user's physical-activity data. Users clip the meter to their clothes or carry it in a pocket, and the sensors detect the duration and intensity of the activity, which are measured in metabolic equivalents (METs)—think of them like horsepower, but for humans instead of cars. It's basically the intensity of your activity. Scientists know the metabolic equivalent for everything from playing basketball (6.5 METs) to chasing wild pigs (3.3 METs). The Centers for Disease Control and Prevention (CDC) recommends that people engage in 60 minutes of moderate to vigorous physical activity each and every day, which means moving at between 3.5 and 11 METs for 60 minutes.

The second part of the system is the Zamzee motivational website, parts of which are shown in Figures 6.1 and 6.2.

Here's how it works. Kids run around all day while wearing their Zamzee meter and then plug their meter into the USB drive on a computer. All their physical-activity data is uploaded to zamzee.com, the website designed in accordance with

Figure 6.1 ZAMZEE AVATAR AND BADGES.
Source: Zamzee, ©2013.

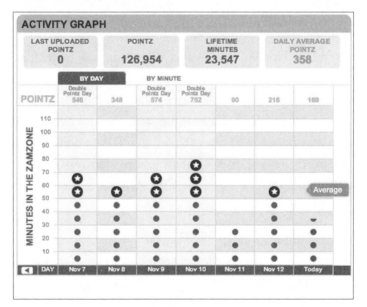

Figure 6.2 ZAMZEE ACTIVITY STATISTICS.
Source: Zamzee, ©2013.

HopeLab's research about what motivates kids to get active and stay active. When kids make it to the ZamZone (a certain MET level), as measured by the Zamzee meter, they start earning Pointz at zamzee.com. Kids also can earn Pointz by uploading their activity consistently, beating their daily average, or being active on surprise double-Pointz days. Other things that kids can do on the website include viewing an activity graph that shows them their activity, customizing their own avatar, leveling up, unlocking badges, and achieving Goalz. Goalz are purchased by parents and put into their kid's Zamzee accounts as a strategic tool to motivate their kids to stay active. For example:

A mom keeping track of her children's activity via their Zamzee accounts notices that her youngest child has been moving less at school recess. She purchases him a $5 Goal to give him extra motivation to move. As he tries to achieve his Goal, he gets back in the habit of regular physical activity at recess.

When kids achieve Goalz, they unlock a spendable currency called Zamz, which then can be spent on a variety of rewards—virtual, tangible, or charitable (Figure 6.3).

Zamzee is designed to jump-start physical activity in kids who may not be naturally inclined to move—and to keep them moving by providing the right combination of incentive and reward. Let's take a look at how the Zamzee experience hits on our intrinsic motivators:

- **Autonomy.** Kids choose how they move with Zamzee. They can decide whether to accept a challenge to escape a T-rex or steer a spaceship away from an alien attack. Then they decide how to move in order to complete that challenge— whether it's running outside with friends or dancing at home in their room. Each choice is equally valid and rewarded.

Figure 6.3 ZAMZEE CHARITABLE-CAUSE REWARDS.
Source: Zamzee, ©2013.

- **Mastery.** Persistence on Zamzee is recognized through collecting badges and passing levels. Whether it takes you a few months or the whole year, everybody has an equal opportunity to reach Level 17: the Zen Master.

- **Purpose.** In addition to badges and levels, rewards add extra incentive for kids to move. Whether it's a donation to a charity or a new pet for their avatar, kids choose what to work toward and focus on achieving it at their own pace.

- **Progress.** Kids can see their activity statistics at any time and have Goalz toward which they can track their progress.

- **Social interaction.** Moving is more fun with friends, which is why kids can friend each other on Zamzee or show their appreciation for a really cool Wham (a status update where you tell everyone else what you did to earn your Pointz) by "liking" it. Families also can keep track of their activity in one place using Family View, making movement a group activity.

Thus far the results have been impressive. Early Zamzee prototypes with minimal gamification elements showed a boost in average activity levels of about 30 percent. With that proof in hand, a more robust Zamzee experience, with additional gamification and Loyalty 3.0 elements, was developed out of HopeLab's research on motivation. This new experience was evaluated recently in a randomized, controlled study conducted by HopeLab with funding from the Robert Wood Johnson Foundation. This research showed an average 59 percent increase in activity among kids using Zamzee compared with a control group. According to HopeLab, this increase is the equivalent of each kid doing an additional 45 minutes of nonstop pushups each week. Or scrubbing floors for three hours a month. Or chasing wild pigs for six minutes a day. Moreover, the increase in activity levels was sustained over a six-month period.

Mathletics!

There's a side benefit to all this gamification and quantification. Kids are using the data from their Zamzee meters to learn math. At Greenfield Hebrew Academy (GHA) middle school in Atlanta, Georgia, they're doing a year-long project in which 126 middle school students and 25 teachers are wearing Zamzee meters all year as part of a school-wide project to jump-start physical activity and collectively reach "a million minutes of activity."

Teachers are then using the Zamzee data in math classes to teach averages, mean, mode, histograms, and other math concepts, and students are learning to use Excel as they calculate the school's goals and track progress.

This is a great example of using Loyalty 3.0 principles to "scaffold" people up to a behavior that they might not normally engage in. Zamzee uses extrinsic motivators as a bridge to the internal motivation, moving kids from, "I know I should be physically active," to, "I'm physically active because it's fun and feels good." In any effort around behavior change, the longer the feedback loop, the harder it is to change the behavior. Exercising for one day isn't going to make someone fit; that person needs to exercise consistently over a period of time in order to see and feel the results. In that period, when the person hasn't yet received the positive reinforcement of feeling fit, there are a lot of opportunities to sit on the couch and eat cupcakes. And with couches and cupcakes, the gratification, is immediate, which makes them much more tempting than the abstract, long-term benefits of "getting fit."

In these scenarios, gamification provides short-term goals and consistent, immediate feedback and positive reinforcement that can keep people on the path to the longer-term goal and help them resist the couches and cupcakes. It shortens the feedback loop.

According to Richard Tate, head of communications and marketing for HopeLab and Zamzee, "We saw from research that gamification and the principles of Loyalty 3.0 can work really well to motivate healthy behavior if thoughtfully applied, and we saw an opportunity to scale that impact with the Zamzee product and business."[2] Zamzee continues to develop new features and functionality for kids and families and is also targeting the health and wellness market through health-care providers, insurers, and others.

- **Concept.** A combination online/offline experience that encourages physical activity

- **Business goals.** Increased, more regular, and more intense physical activity

- **Gamification mechanics.** Transparency, goals, badges, leveling up, competition, community, points

- **Big data.** Online activity, real-world movement, website use, exercise patterns

- **Results.** Increase in physical activity and engagement around exercise

Innovating in Health and Fitness with Loyalty 3.0

Loyalty 3.0 in the exercise space has exploded in recent years with the availability of low-cost sensors and the ubiquity of smart phones (with their own embedded sensors). From big companies such as Nike, with its Nike+ line of products, to device start-ups such as Fitbit and application providers such as Strava, consumers are now able to quantify their physical activity and performance, strive to achieve milestones, compare themselves with others (and their own previous activity), and participate in communities of like-minded enthusiasts. And as sensor technology gets smaller, cheaper, better, and more real time (as well as ingestible, like the sensors from Proteus Digital Health[3]), the immediacy of the feedback and the quantity and granularity of the data will give us more insight into our bodies than ever before. Big data about users' bodies and physical activities, combined with motivation and gamification, enables Loyalty 3.0 to reach into the real world and create meaningful health outcomes.

Getting the Right Exposure to Adobe Photoshop

Suppose that you're an amateur photographer who has just purchased a fancy new camera, and now you want to be able to manipulate all the photos you've taken. You've heard about Photoshop,[4] the powerful image manipulation and modification program from Adobe, and decide to give it a shot. So you download the massive Photoshop 30-day free trial from the Adobe website, then run through the install process, and finally, close to an hour later, launch Photoshop. And what do you see? A blank white canvas and a mind-boggling assortment of menus, panels, and buttons. It's daunting, to say the least. You don't know what the important stuff is or where to find it. You have no idea where to start.

Many people will stop right there — not knowing what to do, not gaining any understanding of what Photoshop is capable of, and most concerning for Adobe, not buying Photoshop when the 30-day trial is up. Contrast this with the out-of-box-experience of any recent video game. While the interface might be as complex (if not more so) than Photoshop, game designers long ago learned how to onboard their users. Rather than throwing big manuals at them (and expecting that people will read them) or signing them up for training courses, *they enable users to learn the game by playing the game.* By giving users a set of progressively harder tasks to accomplish, giving them the time and freedom to explore, practice, and make mistakes, and revealing more complex concepts over time, they onboard users quickly and in a way that engages users and gives them a sense of accomplishment and mastery. Confident in their newfound knowledge, players then can jump into the game in earnest.

Adobe was well aware of its "out-of-box-experience" problem and funded a series of internal lab experiments to try to solve it.

The experiments, initially conceived by Petar Karafezov, Adobe Creative Suite digital marketing manager, started with creating an onboarding experience inspired by video games.

"It was a joke at first," Karafezov commented—but eventually he secured the internal funding at Adobe to develop the mission-oriented onboarding tool now known as LevelUp for Photoshop. As you'll see, the concept is highly useful for any complex piece of software, complex processes such as doing your taxes, or anywhere you need to engage and motivate learners through a path to mastery.

LevelUp for Photoshop was designed as a plugin for Photoshop that both free-trial and existing users can download and install. After installation, the LevelUp plugin is available directly within Photoshop, and when launched, it invites users to start playing.

LevelUp consists of 12 missions, each of which exposes users to a critical piece of functionality within Photoshop and which are sequenced in order of difficulty (Figure 6.4). To complete a mission, a user has to learn about one or more features of Photoshop and practice them on either one of his own photos or one provided as part of the LevelUp plugin.

The missions are split across three levels, and users can't do any of the level 2 missions until they have completed all the level 1 missions (and mastered all the corresponding functionality)—hence the name *LevelUp*. This is often referred to as *progressive disclosure*—only showing the user what's directly appropriate for him to see and interact with at any point in time. Seeing Mission 12 when you're just starting out isn't appropriate, but it is by the time you've reached level 3. Along with the short goals presented by each mission, the levels also create longer goals, both for the achievement of leveling up and also for unlocking new, harder missions.

LEVEL 1	
Mission One	Remove red eye from a photo
Mission Two	Improve a smile by whitening teeth
Mission Three	Smooth a face
Mission Four	Remove unwanted objects
LEVEL 2	
Mission Five	Straighten a photo
Mission Six	Cut an object out of a photo
Mission Seven	Recompose an image
Mission Eight	Darken or lighten areas of an image
LEVEL 3	
Mission Nine	Add a new background to an image
Mission Ten	Replace colors in an image
Mission Eleven	Create a perfect group portrait
Mission Twelve	Create a composite image

Figure 6.4 LEVELUP FOR PHOTOSHOP MISSIONS.
Source: Adobe, Inc.

Within each mission, the user is given a task to accomplish, for instance, to whiten teeth in a photo (Figure 6.5). Instead of the traditional learning model of "learn, then do," LevelUp flips the model around and asks the user to accomplish a task at the outset. It's "do, then learn."

If the user has the requisite skill and knowledge (or is just good at figuring things out), he can go ahead and complete the task. If not, the plugin walks him through the required steps and optionally points him to tutorial text and video content to provide in-depth training. This is the same educational content that has always been there, by the way, but that hasn't been compelling for trial users to engage with. They just want to get in and manipulate photos, not go through training!

In this case, though, the learning is directed. The user has a very specific task that he's trying to accomplish, and the learn-

Figure 6.5 YOUR MISSION SHOULD YOU CHOOSE TO ACCEPT IT: WHITEN TEETH.
Source: Molly Kittle.

ing is focused specifically on that task. I'm an engineer, and when I learn a new programming language, I don't just pick up and read a book on the programming language. I have a project in mind, and I learn the language with that project in mind—so all my learning is in service of the task I'm trying to accomplish. That makes the learning much more compelling and engaging because by learning, I'm figuring out how to accomplish my goals.

Users earn points at the completion of every mission and bonus points for unlocking badges that indicate special milestones or accomplishments, such as the "Deadeye" badge for removing red-eye with a single click per eye, the "Surgeon General" badge for cutting out an object quickly, and the "Dentariste" badge for whitening teeth with a single click (Figure 6.6). Users can track their progress through each level with a clearly visible progress bar.

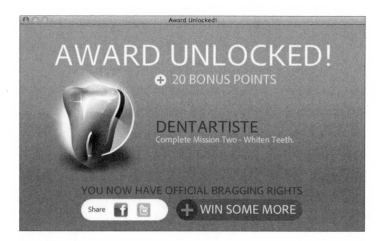

Figure 6.6 THE "DENTARTISTE" BADGE.
Source: Adobe, Inc

Users can share their progress and badges to their social networks on Facebook and Twitter, and a web page on adobe.com features a weekly leaderboard showing who has earned the most points, as well as a live news feed of recent user activity. When users complete the 12 missions, they have mastered key Photoshop functionality and have successfully "leveled up" their skills.

To evaluate the success of LevelUp, Adobe used four sources of data:

- User-activity data from the LevelUp plugin
- User surveys conducted on a monthly basis
- In-depth interviews with a small group of users
- Data from the Adobe Product Improvement Program, an opt-in program that tracks how Adobe Photoshop users use the software

According to Adobe research scientist Mira Dontcheva, from this mix of qualitative and quantitative data, Adobe learned:

- That the step-by-step nature of LevelUp helped users to focus on one tool at a time rather than being overwhelmed by the entire interface.

- How users worked their way through the missions, where they were spending a lot of time, and where they were quitting and never coming back. By using this data, Adobe was able to adjust the mission difficulty to reduce user drop-off.

- That although the points could be redeemed for prizes, that wasn't the primary motivator for many people to go through LevelUp. The prizes were available only to users in the United States and Canada, but as many as 60 percent of the players were from other countries, and plugin installation rates remained constant even in months without prizes. Mastery was the clear driver here, with autonomy, purpose, and progress playing strong supporting roles.

- That users enjoyed the experience and learned something in the process. Survey results indicated that more than 90 percent agreed or strongly agreed to the statement, "I enjoyed playing the game." Almost 90 percent agreed or strongly agreed to the statement, "The game helped me learn something new." And almost 85 percent agreed or strongly agreed to the statement, "I learned the basics of photo editing using Photoshop."

- That based on analyzing before and after data from the Adobe Product Improvement Program, all users, regardless of their experience level, learned new features that they hadn't used prior to LevelUp. Often these tools or workflows had been in the product for several years, but experienced users had missed them as they upgraded. Users had comments such as, "Even though I have been using Photoshop for just over six years, there are some little tips and tricks that I never knew about," and, "I found this game to fill in some of the stuff I should have learned and been using but somehow missed while learning."

Adobe found that not only did LevelUp for Photoshop get more people up the learning curve faster and using more tools and workflows than before, but it also got more prospective customers to buy the product after trying it. At the end of the day, LevelUp helped Adobe users and Adobe, Inc., itself in four ways:

1. **Sales.** Customers could feel confident in their ability to use Photoshop before buying it.

2. **Training.** Missions guided new customers through a carefully planned skill sequence.

3. **Discovery.** Missions encouraged existing users to acquire new skills.

4. **Reference.** Existing users could refer back to a mission for a refresher or enhancer on a particular skill or workflow—one of the benefits of an interactive tutorial where users can use their own photos.

According to Tacy Trowbridge, worldwide leader for education programs, Adobe plans a deeper and wider application of Loyalty 3.0 to onboarding and beyond. The company plans to go *wider* by leveraging Loyalty 3.0 principles in other products in its creative suite, such as Adobe Illustrator and Adobe InDesign. The company plans to go *deeper* by expanding the application of Loyalty 3.0 along several fronts, including:

• Creating communities where users are rewarded for helping onboard other users, as well as sharing tips and techniques

• Creating "challenge rounds" where users can test their skills on a new set of images, get community feedback on their modified image, vote on the best image, and so on

- Enabling nonprofits and charities to submit projects into the LevelUp framework that users then can use their newly learned skills to complete

- Empowering community members to extend and enhance the LevelUp experience with their own missions, levels, and tutorials

- Empowering educators to extend and enhance the Level Up experience to address their specific educational curriculums and needs

- Enabling users to earn official skill certifications by completing LevelUp missions

In summary, it's clear that Adobe didn't turn learning Photoshop into Angry Birds. The company simply reframed its existing tutorial content with gamification using nine of ten of the gamification mechanics that we identified in Chapter 4 (the only one missing, for the moment, is collaboration). Then the company took the data generated from the LevelUp plugin and combined it with the big data from the Adobe Product Improvement Program and the qualitative data from user surveys and interviews to develop deeper insight into its users and products and light the way toward future product developments.

- **Concept.** A complex piece of software that uses the onboarding and training techniques from video games to quickly get new users trained and feeling a sense of confidence and mastery

- **Business goals.** Onboard new customers quickly so that they feel confident enough in their abilities to buy the product and teach existing customers new tools and workflows, as well as old ones they may have missed, so that they're more likely to continue using Photoshop versus any competing products

- **Gamification mechanics.** Fast feedback, transparency, goals, badges, leveling up, onboarding, competition, community, points

- **Big data.** User activity, purchase, product-improvement program

- **Results.** Increased sales, new users learning product, existing users learning new features and workflows, all users enjoying the experience; Adobe learned more about how its customers like to learn and what they're doing with Photoshop

Clippy's Second Chance: Microsoft Ribbon Hero 2

Adobe isn't the only company to market powerful software. Microsoft Office is an entire suite of feature-rich products, including the familiar Word, Excel, PowerPoint, and One-Note, among others. Office is a multi-billion-dollar business for Microsoft, so it is in the company's best interest for its users (especially the Generation Y users, who have no history with Office) to understand the breadth and depth of functionality available in the software suite. Otherwise, those same users might defect to cheaper, "good enough" alternatives such as Google Docs or the free Office Web Apps.

As a consequence Microsoft built Ribbon Hero (a play on Guitar Hero), a plugin for Office and Microsoft's first foray into using gamification to motivate users to learn its products. The results were intriguing enough that the company subsequently released Ribbon Hero 2, which wrapped the entire experience in a story and required users to use all the products in the suite (Figure 6.7). The company does a great job of describing the plugin on the Ribbon Hero 2 website:

Welcome to Ribbon Hero 2![4]

You've tried games that test your card playing, your imaginary farming skills, and your ability to hurl small birds. Finally there's a game that will make you better at your job.

Do you feel like you're using Word, Excel, PowerPoint, and OneNote the same way version after version, or have you avoided using one of these apps because you don't know how? And you know there's so much more Office could be doing for you if only you knew how to access it? No more! Straight from the secret lairs of Office Labs we present Ribbon Hero 2: Clippy's Second Chance.[5] Yes, we turned Office into a game! If you're going to spend time immersed in the inner workings of Office, by golly it should be fun. In Ribbon Hero 2, you'll hop on board Clippy's stolen time machine and explore different time periods. With each time period, you get to explore a new game board with challenges you must complete to get to the next level. Each challenge takes you into Word, Excel,

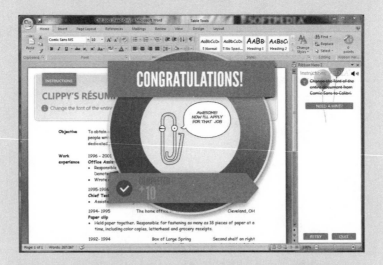

Figure 6.7 RIBBON HERO 2—COMPLETING THE FIRST MISSION.
Source: Used with permission from Microsoft.

PowerPoint, or OneNote to complete a task. Discover new Office features by actually using them, with a hint button to fall back on in case you get stuck. Race for a high score with colleagues, classmates and friends, or even put your score on your résumé to show off your Office skills!

For those of you who have been paying attention, we've done this before. That's how we got the "2" on the end of the title. So what's different? *deep breath* Clippy, comic strips, colorful graphics, surprise animations, multiple levels, time travel, upside-down Clippy, space ships, Greek Gods, bow-and-arrow battles, and a ton of useful Office features.

Gearing Up with Ford of Canada

You're looking for a new car, so you pay a visit to your local Ford of Canada dealership.[6] The salesperson welcomes you warmly, asks thoughtful questions about what you're looking for, and then shows you the cars that meet your needs. She demos the latest in-car technology features for you, and she answers all your questions quickly and efficiently. She seems to know every last detail about the cars that she's showing you, and she can even tell you how Ford cars stack up against the competition. When it comes time to introduce you to a financing manager, she makes the transition flawlessly and leaves you amazed at how competently, confidently, and professionally she handled your experience.

If you're Ford Motor Company of Canada, this is exactly how you want your customer buying experience to be. In order to deliver it, though, you need a way to train, motivate, and support your sales and service employees on everything from new-car features, to in-car technology, to financing plans, and the desired customer experience.

Working with its long-time partner, Maritz Canada, Ford of Canada created the Professional Performance Program (p^2p). According to Rob Pearson, vice president of customer experience at Maritz Canada, "p^2p is a digital destination where sales and service staff from Ford stores across Canada have access to online product and service training, sales resources, certification, and reward and recognition. It enables and motivates sales and service staff to deliver a customer experience that is aligned with the Ford brand and consistently outstanding."

The p^2p portal had been very successful in the past, with great employee:

- **Satisfaction.** The satisfaction rate for the existing experience was a very impressive 92 percent.
- **Awareness.** Eighty-five percent of dealership personnel were meeting training requirements.
- **Effectiveness.** All Ford's performance measures were higher for certified versus noncertified participants.

The challenge that the company was facing was how to innovate in an already successful program to drive even better results. Enter Loyalty 3.0. The company's main goals in implementing Loyalty 3.0 principles into the p^2p portal were to:

- Drive site traffic.
- Combat underutilization of valuable resources.
- Encourage informal and formal learning.
- Turn, "I use p^2p because I *have* to," into, "I use p^2p because I *want* to."

Working together, Maritz Canada and Ford of Canada created the Ford p^2p Cup (Figure 6.8), a program themed around professional motor racing that motivates sales and service representatives to learn more by browsing the p²p portal, watching informational videos, downloading and consuming the latest product information, and taking web courses. Participants can earn RPMs (points) and Gear Up (level up), work toward individual goals, earn badges that are visible in a trophy case, compete with their peers on leaderboards, work together to accomplish team goals, compete against other dealerships, and receive real-time feedback as they engage in the desired behavior.

After introducing Loyalty 3.0 principles into p²p, Ford of Canada saw the following results:

- There was a 417 percent increase in site usage versus the same period the previous year.

- Within the first three months of the program, the site exceeded the traffic volume of the entire previous year.

- There were 15 percent more unique visitors and a 30 percent increase in unique visits versus the same period the previous year.

Figure 6.8 THE FORD p²p CUP.
Source: Maritz Canada.

- A positive correlation was seen between engagement in the Ford p²p Cup and key performance measures, including sales and customer satisfaction.

- There was increased engagement by younger audiences, which represented 40 percent of the total audience, in the Ford p²p Cup.

- There was an increase in volunteer learning—participants completing courses above and beyond what they were required to do for their annual certification requirements.

- There was a month-over-month increase in engagement with the program as word of mouth spread among the sales and service community.

One of the participants in the program had this to say: "I have been with Ford for 13 years and have found so much more information or a way to get that information just by 'playing.' I never realized that we were able to access the information that we can."

According to Pearson, the other major benefit of the program has been a change in perception of the p²p portal—from a place where participants just go to get certified to a place where they go to share ideas, engage in more informal learning, and participate in a learning community.

Ford of Canada's p²p program is a great example of how Loyalty 3.0 principles can enhance an experience, even if the program is already very successful, and drive key performance metrics while motivating and engaging participants.

- **Concept.** A learning program designed to encourage certification, use of content, and informal learning as well as to drive job performance

- **Business goals.** Drive site traffic, increase use of content, decrease time to certification, and encourage learning

- **Gamification mechanics.** Fast feedback, transparency, goals, badges, leveling up, competition, collaboration, community, points
- **Big data.** User activity, content consumption, employee performance, customer satisfaction, course completion
- **Results.** Increased engagement, sales and customer satisfaction, increased learning, increased resource use, creation of a culture of learning

Innovating in Education with Loyalty 3.0

Imagine a game where for three to six months you do a bunch of learning and work that you don't know the purpose of (Why am I learning about arctangents again?), and at the end of it, you get a single letter that tells you how you did. And then you do it again, and again, for years. At the end, that collection of letters determines your future. Sound like the worst game ever?

Indeed it is, and yet it's how we expect students to learn today. Abstract goals (letter grades), long feedback loops (quarters and semesters), purposeless work (Why do I care about arctangents?), and an unclear sense of progress (Where am I in the big scheme of things?) all serve to demotivate students and turn school and learning into a grind for many. Faced with this problem, several companies, startups, and forward-thinking educators are starting to look at gamification and Loyalty 3.0 principles as a way to drive engagement with learning.

Learning at Scale with Khan Academy

The Khan Academy[7] is a not-for-profit created in 2006 that aims to provide "a free world-class education for anyone anywhere." The website features thousands of videos on topics from K–12 math, to biology, to finance; automated exercises that adapt to the learner; and a map of knowledge that learners can traverse with autonomy. At Khan Academy, gamification is used to motivate and engage learners—to give them challenges, immediate feedback, and a continual sense of progress and purpose. In addition, with over 200 million lessons delivered, Khan Academy has a vast stream of big data to analyze how individuals, classrooms, and their entire community are learning, and the academy can use this information to optimize not only its gamification implementation but also its core product and content.

The Multiplayer Classroom

"Good morning. Welcome to the first class of the semester. Everyone in this class is going to receive an F." That's how Professor Lee Sheldon of the Rensselaer Polytechnic Institute starts off his class every quarter. Once students have had a few seconds to absorb that zinger, he continues, "Unless . . . " At which point he explains to them what they'll need to accomplish in the class, framing everything in the language of multiplayer games—working on projects, taking tests, and working together as teams become "embark on quests, defeat boss monsters, and work with your guild." And if the students do well, they'll level up, possibly even to an A. As Sheldon writes in his book, *The Multiplayer Classroom: Designing Coursework as a Game*, "There was an immediate and perceptible shift in the room from shock to interest, and something more: challenge."[8]

Translating the Web with Duolingo

Duolingo[9] is a free service that helps you learn languages while simultaneously translating real-world content from the Internet. Duolingo was started by Carnegie Mellon professor Luis von Ahn, a pioneer in the field of *human computation* who also created reCAPTCHA (where you have to type in the squiggly words to prove that you're a human on a website and at the same time you're helping to digitize the text of books) and the ESP Game (where two randomly paired people are shown a picture and have to use the same word to describe it in order to "win" and at the same time they're labeling pictures so that search engines can find them). Participants in Duolingo work their way through a skill tree (Figure 6.9), earn skill points, compare their skill ranking with that of others, and can track their progress over time. By once again approaching a large-scale problem (translating the web) as a human computation problem, von Ahn and Duolingo have created an experience that benefits individuals as well as society. Much like learning how to use Photoshop, there's an intrinsic desire among the

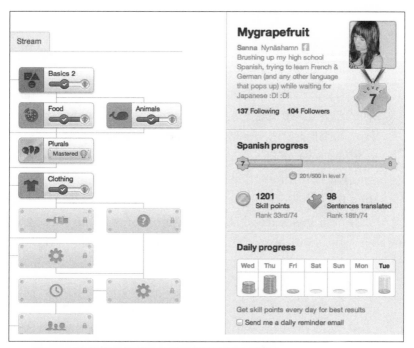

Figure 6.9 THE DUOLINGO SPANISH SKILL TREE.
Source: Duolingo.com, ©2013.

participants to want to learn, but the process can be challenging. By integrating gamification into the experience, Duolingo
is able to motivate users to continually move forward on their
path to mastery.

Just Press Play

Particularly in a university setting, education isn't just about
the content and the learning. It's also about making friends,
developing support networks of peers and professors, knowing
and being comfortable in your surroundings, and feeling like
you belong and are part of a community. Without these things,
students can feel disconnected, demotivated, and disengaged
and are at risk for failure and attrition.

Just Press Play[10] is a program created and run at the Rochester Institute of Technology (RIT) in New York to address just
this issue among the 720 undergraduate students in the School
of Interactive Games and Media. Participants in Just Press Play
are given goals and earn achievements (badges) for completing tasks such as visiting the offices of faculty members (and
accomplishing a mission while there, such as making the professor laugh or dancing for her in order to build a personal connection), participating in flash mobs, eating off campus with a
group of 12 or more friends, exploring a new part of campus, or
attending a lecture.

These goals are all based on foundational attributes that
have been proven to help students succeed in the long run.
"What games tend to be really good at is giving you a big-pic-
ture view of things, how things fit together and the milestones
along the way," says Elizabeth Lawley, professor of interactive
games and media and head of production for Just Press Play.
"For our students, the dragon to be slain is graduating, and getting the job is the pot of gold. But students don't always see

what we see, which is that it's the things that happen along the journey that make them able to slay the dragon."[11]

There are also ways for the community to work together to accomplish shared goals. At the end of a recent quarter, the designers created a goal and badge for everyone in the program that would be earned if 90 percent of the freshmen in certain specialties passed their first programming class. This shared responsibility and accountability motivated the upperclassmen to engage with the freshmen to the point where they independently organized a weekend study session just to help them.

The Just Press Play program at RIT engages students in a program that has nothing to do with grades or class credit but everything to do with their long-term success. By encouraging students to network, explore, help each other, and bond, the program builds the foundation and support networks that enable students not only to survive but also to thrive.

Wrapping It Up

Now that you're exercising regularly, have mastered Adobe Photoshop, are speaking fluent Spanish, and can describe the safety features on a Ford Escape, it's time to look at our final set of case studies—how Loyalty 3.0 is being used to engage and motivate employees.

CHAPTER 7

Case Studies in Employee Engagement

Throughout this book we've talked about the idea that it isn't just customers who can benefit from Loyalty 3.0 principles but also employees. Businesses know that they need to counter the effects of employee disengagement and that anything they can do to motivate training and development, collaboration, and job performance will have a significant business impact.

In 2000, *HBR OnPoint* published an article titled, "Putting the Service-Profit Chain to Work,"[1] that very clearly articulated the value of employee engagement and loyalty, which I'll adapt slightly here:

- Employee engagement drives employee satisfaction.

- Employee satisfaction drives loyalty.

- Employee loyalty drives productivity.

- Employee productivity drives value.

- Value drives customer satisfaction.

- Customer satisfaction drives customer loyalty.

- Customer loyalty drives profitability and growth.

So the key to profitability and growth is employee engagement. And in this chapter we're going to see how Loyalty 3.0 in the workplace can be used to activate employee engagement, performance, and motivation at scale while at the same time accomplishing business goals.

Inspiring Agents with LiveOps

Imagine that you have 20,000 people working for you, from their homes around the country, in bunny slippers, as independent customer-service agents. Okay, maybe they're not all wearing bunny slippers, but the question remains: How do you engage and motivate this highly distributed workforce of independent agents?

LiveOps,[2] a provider of cloud-based contact-center technology and talent, faced just this issue, and the company knew that it needed to innovate to address it. The company's 20,000 agents were handling customer service for firms such as Symantec, Royal Mail Group, and AAA, and LiveOps wanted to drive great customer satisfaction and outcomes for its clients. As early adopters of consumer technology in its distributed workforce (Remember how corporate IT is being consumerized from Chapter 1?), the company was one of the first businesses to recognize the value of Loyalty 3.0 inside the enterprise.

LiveOps has a unique and interesting business model. Its distributed workforce has no managers and no standard business hours, and its independent agents have complete *autonomy* over their interactions with the company. Every week agents can bid for work, which they receive based on their skills, historical performance, and work availability. LiveOps provides them with complete *transparency* into their performance and lets agents make their own choices about how to achieve client mandates. According to Sanjay Mathur, vice president of product management at LiveOps in an article on the Management

Innovation eXchange (MIX), "We find that agents who have control of how they work are inherently more inspired brand ambassadors, and this carries through to customer satisfaction and outcomes for their clients. We don't supervise, we inspire!"

Agents *compete* against each other for work, which drives them to perform to the best of their abilities. But it's not a zero-sum game with a fixed amount of work to go around. The better that client expectations are met by the collective LiveOps community, the more business those clients give to LiveOps and, by extension, the entire community. So agents help other agents through informal channels, as well as through knowledge bases, forums, and tools that LiveOps provides for peer coaching and networking. By *collaborating* and sharing best practices and tips, agents develop bonds with other agents and reputation in the LiveOps community, and the entire community collectively benefits with more work.

In 2009, LiveOps added gamification to its online agent portal, My Work Community. Agents earn points by hitting performance goals, completing certifications, and interacting with the community and then can spend those points to customize an avatar that represents their method of identity and reputation in the community. They also can spend points on more tangible rewards, such as the right to apply for certain opportunities within LiveOps. Badges signify accomplished training and performance goals, real-time feedback reinforces positive agent behavior, and leaderboards and a profile page with detailed agent statistics enable agents to know how they're doing individually as well as in relation to the rest of the community.

"It gets them to look at what they are doing and how to improve. And it allows our contractors to see how they are performing against their peers," Mathur says. "We are trying to motivate them to know where they stand and decide what they can do to improve. What's interesting for us is the alignment of gamification with performance."[3]

Following the launch of gamification in LiveOps' My Work Community:

- Eighty percent of agents opted into the gamification program, with 75 percent of them returning on a biweekly basis.

- Certification, motivated with gamification mechanics (although that wasn't required), was completed by 72 percent of agents. So much like we saw with Ford of Canada, there was an increase in *volunteer learning*.

- The onboarding process for agents dropped from four weeks of classroom training to 14 hours.

- There was an improvement in service levels of about 10 percent.

- There was an almost 15 percent reduction in the average time to handle a customer inquiry.

- There was an 8 to 12 percent improvement in sales performance.[4]

By adopting Loyalty 3.0 principles in its agent community, LiveOps has been able to drive significant business results around agent engagement, motivation, and performance, resulting in better outcomes for its clients.

- **Concept.** An employee community designed to motivate and engage a distributed workforce to learn and perform better

- **Business goals.** Train agents faster, increase their performance, and engage them in a distributed community

- **Gamification mechanics.** Fast feedback, transparency,

goals, badges, onboarding, competition, collaboration, community, points

- **Big data.** User activity, service levels, call times, sales performance, onboarding times
- **Results.** Decreased onboarding time, increased customer satisfaction, decreased average call time, increased sales

Working the Crowd with CrowdFlower

I mentioned CrowdFlower in Chapter 3 when I discussed crowdsourcing. It's the company that has access to over 2.5 million on-demand workers around the world to whom it can farm out *microtasks* (such as checking to see if an image is offensive or detecting the sentiment of a forum post). As you might imagine, like LiveOps, engaging and motivating this diverse, distributed workforce is a challenge, as is ensuring superior-quality work at the company's large scale. In 2012, the company launched a worker motivation program aimed at improving work quality and the satisfaction of its online workforce. By gamifying the CrowdFlower dashboard, used by contributors hired to solve a problem or complete a microtask, CrowdFlower encourages and rewards superior work and accuracy. And by tracking badges earned by top contributors, CrowdFlower is able to offer better workers higher-paying projects.

Preventing Death by PowerPoint with BOX

Doug Landis, vice president of sales productivity at fast-growing cloud services provider BOX, was planning the company's BOX 2012 sales conference. He wanted the conference to be memorable and valuable. "I was adamant that I didn't want our sales team to succumb to that dreaded affliction of conference-goers everywhere: death by PowerPoint," Landis commented in a guest blog post written for Bunchball.

Here's the rest of the blog post,[5] which describes a unique application of Loyalty 3.0:

> *You know what I mean. Endless slides, presenters droning on and on, dim lighting enveloping a jet-lagged audience fighting to stay awake. No good ever comes from pummeling your best people into a slide-induced coma. And if you bore them to death, they're not likely to take in and retain the information you plan to deliver.*
>
> *So this year we were determined to host an event that combined real learning with the engagement and relevance of a mobile-oriented experience. Upping the ante for our sales event was imperative for three main reasons:*
>
> 1. ***We're a fast-growing company***, *and that sometimes makes it difficult for new and existing employees to get to know one another. We had to make it easy for people to network, and we wanted those meetings to be fun, interesting and memorable.*
>
> 2. ***We had a lot of material to cover*** *at the conference. But we're not a boring company, and our culture is anything but. So though we had lots of knowledge to transfer, a straight-up day of lectures wasn't going to cut it.*
>
> 3. ***Sales people are competitive by nature.*** *The more we could harness that trait, the more they'd engage, and the more fun they'd have.*

Looking at that list, we thought, "Why not gamify our sales conference? Companies gamify websites and applications and programs, so why not our event?"

It struck us as a perfect way to add a new dimension to the sales meeting experience. And a gamified event is great fit for the BOX culture, which encourages a spirit of cooperative competition, or "coopetition."

Here are some highlights:

It started with check-in. *Using their mobile devices, all our attendees checked in to the conference and instantly became part of the gamification experience.*

We turned learning into a competition. *The day featured five conference sessions. To confirm that our content was gaining traction with sales team members, we had everyone answer questions on key points that were covered in each session—five questions per session, 25 questions in all, and they earned points for every correct answer. The points provided a vehicle for competition, and we set it up so everyone could compete both individually and in teams. Participants checked their standing—and that of their team—on a real-time leaderboard. Checking the leaderboard let participants see who had the best shot at winning several top prizes.*

We made a game of networking. *Gamification offered uniquely fun and effective ways to establish personal connections between team members who might not have the chance to meet otherwise. Earning points for finding the answers to "Fun Facts"* *trivia questions about colleagues (Which one was a White House intern? Who gave will.i.am a bloody nose playing softball?) motivated participants to get to know each other. The result was a much more entertaining, effective team building experience than what you get in the typical sales meeting setting.*

Everybody got in the game. *To get the results we wanted, everybody needed to participate. But people carry all kinds of phones and devices—iOS, Android, BlackBerry, etc.—so to make sure everyone had access to the experience, we needed something that worked like an app but didn't care what platform you used. Writing different apps for multiple platforms wasn't feasible for a one-day event, so we worked with a partner and created an intuitive, push-button mobile experience delivered through an optimized mobile website. It was platform-neutral and still had the look, feel and responsiveness of an app.*

Gamifying the event helped us fully engage every single sales rep from the moment they arrived at the conference until we wrapped it up. We received excellent feedback on the mobile experience from our team, and I know for a fact that our people internalized the material we presented far more effectively than if we had just served up the usual buffet of presentation slides.

Finally, there's a cure for death by PowerPoint. And its name is Gamification.

- **Concept.** A single-use application for conferences, designed to engage attendees with the content and encourage networking with each other

- **Business goals.** Better sales performance because salespeople learned what they needed to at the kickoff event; better internal collaboration because salespeople got to know each other

- **Gamification mechanics.** Fast feedback, transparency, competition, collaboration, community, points

- **Big data.** User activity

- **Results.** Engaged salespeople, content internalized more effectively, new connections made

Going Social with Bluewolf

Most businesses have a huge, untapped marketing asset at their disposal—their employees. What if you could motivate every one of your employees to post to their personal and professional networks about your latest product, your newest promotional offer, or the latest deep thoughts on your corporate blog? Think about how your marketing efforts would be amplified just by getting the people who work for you to help make your business—which is really *their* business—more successful. Bluewolf,[6] a 500+ person global business consulting firm, decided to use Loyalty 3.0 principles to give all of its employees a megaphone and to encourage them to use it.

Most consultancies are black boxes They don't want their employees exposed to the outside world, which might open them up to being recruited by competitors, and they don't want to share their hard-earned knowledge because they consider it a part of their competitive advantage. Bluewolf took the opposite tack and decided that it wanted all of its consultants to freely and openly share their knowledge and establish their own brands in the market. Corinne Sklar, Bluewolf's chief marketing officer, believed that doing so would educate the company's

Figure 7.1 BLUEWOLF'S #goingsocial.
Source: Bluewolf, ©2013.

client base, establish Bluewolf's expertise and reputation, and serve to drive new business. To implement this transparency and sharing, Bluewolf built the #goingsocial program (Figure 7.1), which consists of three parts:

1. **Pack profiles.** Every consultant has a public profile on the Bluewolf website, the content of which is a mix of automated data and data explicitly entered by the consultant, which includes the consultant's areas of expertise, recent tweets, certifications, blog posts, and links to content the consul-

tant has authored. All the data that consultants publish to their Pack Profile is entered into Bluewolf's salesforce.com deployment and then pushed to the public website. This enables Bluewolf to track every time a consultant submits a piece of content. Then, using web analytics tools, Bluewolf is also able to detect every time a consultant's profile or one of the consultant's pieces of authored content is viewed so that it can track and reward not only content creation but also popularity.

2. **#goingsocial portal.** With new sites coming and going all the time and unclear rules of engagement about how to represent your business on social media, it was clear to Bluewolf that it needed to educate its consultants on how to get started and most effectively use social media, including platforms such as Facebook, LinkedIn, Salesforce Chatter, Google+, and Pinterest. The #goingsocial portal provides slide presentations and short video tutorials to quickly get employees up to speed.

3. **Gamification.** To encourage consultants to use their new-found voices, Bluewolf uses gamification in its salesforce.com deployment to motivate consultants to create, share, and drive traffic to content. Consultants compete with each other to see who can be the most social and can re-deem the points they earn for experiential rewards such as dinner with the CEO or being showcased by Bluewolf in social media, as well as dollar-value rewards such as Blue-wolf clothing or upgrades on flights.

The program has resulted in substantial increases in social sharing, with traffic to Bluewolf's blogs from social-media platforms increasing by 153 percent and traffic to its website increasing by 68 percent. By analyzing the incoming data, Bluewolf is able to determine which social-media platforms result in the most traffic, as well as the highest rate of conversion into customers, and can optimize its gamification program accordingly to drive the maximum benefit. In addition to the jump in external activity, Bluewolf also has seen a 57 percent increase in activity in Salesforce Chatter, the firm's internal collaboration network, and an eightfold increase in the size of the Bluewolf blogger community. By using Loyalty 3.0 principles to educate its employees and then to amplify their voices through social media, Bluewolf has turned its employee base into engaged advocates, increased the profile of its thought leaders, and driven more traffic to the company's properties.

- **Concept.** A social-media education and amplification program for employees
- **Business goals.** Establish Bluewolf consultants as thought leaders and trusted advisors, drive traffic to the company's web properties, source new business
- **Gamification mechanics.** Fast feedback, transparency, goals, badges, leveling up, onboarding, competition, community, points
- **Big data.** User activity, web analytics, traffic sources, social-media sharing
- **Results.** Increase in the number of employees customizing their profiles and blogging, increase in internal collaboration, increase in traffic to company's blog, increase in traffic to company's website

Innovating in Reputation with Loyalty 3.0

What's your reputation? At home, at work, and in your local community? *Merriam-Webster's Dictionary* defines *reputation* as "overall quality or character as seen or judged by people in general" and "recognition by other people of some characteristic or ability."[7] Note that this definition makes clear that your reputation depends on other people and is therefore something over which you have only indirect control. Reputation is, by nature, an informal and qualitative attribute. As we live more of our lives online, however, some of this informal, qualitative reputation can be formalized and quantified. J. P. Rangaswami, chief scientist at salesforce.com, recognizes three different kinds of reputation:

- **Asserted.** I say that I'm good at something, such as, "I'm the best chef in California." The credibility of this statement is directly correlated with my credibility on this topic, which you may or may not know. There is also only a single data point—this is my opinion about me.

- **Bestowed.** Someone else says that I'm good at something, such as, "He's the best chef in California." The credibility of this statement is directly correlated with the credibility of the person who makes it and that person's credibility on this particular topic, which you may or may not know. By default, it has more credibility than anything I have asserted myself because it's coming from a third party with an assumed lack of vested interest. One benefit of a bestowed reputation is that you can have multiple data points because multiple people can say that you're good at something, giving you a higher confidence level.

- **Earned.** An unbiased test or statistic says that I'm good at something or have done something, such as, "He passed the California Master Chef exam." This is the only objective component of the three, and the most credible, although you may not know whether the California Master Chef exam is easy or hard. Here also you have the benefit of multiple data points—if the user passed two other tests in addition to the California Master Chef exam, that gives you a higher confidence level that the person actually is a master chef.

Any *one* of these types of reputations has its weaknesses. You can't always believe what people say about themselves, but others might not know about characteristics or abilities that they have, so how else are you going to find out about them? You can't always believe what others say about someone because they might just be being nice for fear of offending or hoping for a reciprocal gesture, or they might not know anything about the topic—all sorts of social dynamics come into play here. And you can't rely on objective tests for everything because (1) all tests are created by someone and are therefore subjective to at least some degree, and (2) you can't make tests on everything—it's too much work.

But when you start combining these components, it starts to get interesting, and you get a deeper, richer view on reputation. Before you can access this view, you first need employees to take the time and energy to assert things about themselves, bestow skills and characteristics on others, and earn reputations by accomplishing tasks or taking tests. This is where Loyalty 3.0 comes in. In fact, several of the Loyalty 3.0 examples that we've looked at have reputation at their core, either implicitly (it's part of the system but not called out as such) or explicitly. In the SAP Community Network, for example, you develop an explicit reputation based on the content that you've contributed (earned) and that other people have shared, liked, and downloaded (bestowed)—a reputation that has a meaningful career impact. Employing more formalized reputation systems for employees at work also can yield numerous benefits. In a time when our work is being mediated by technology, workforces are distributed and remote, and employees who have never met each other are working together in online collaboration networks, an employee reputation system is necessary to get work done efficiently and effectively. In particular, employee reputation systems enable businesses to do the following in an automated and scalable way:

- Identify skill gaps and develop employees.
- Establish a measurement framework that can be used:
  - To objectively compare employees.
  - To give employees transparency into their performance.
  - By employees as goals to work toward.
- Benchmark both internally and externally.
- Identify centers of expertise and distribute that knowledge.
- Socialize employee achievements automatically.
- Use the right people for the right job.
- Assemble high-performance teams.

With Loyalty 3.0-powered reputation, every employee has a "baseball card," and every manager has the information she needs to field a competitive team and win.

Turbocharging Sales with Nitro for Salesforce

Salesforce.com is a global enterprise software company with more than 100,000 customers, best known for its sales force automation (SFA) product that enables sales professionals to manage all phases of the sales process from lead management, to analytics, to forecasting. A pioneer in cloud computing, where all the software is hosted and run from the company's data centers and is accessible over the public Internet, salesforce.com's products are quick to deploy and are purchased on a subscription basis [often referred to as *software as a service* (SaaS)].

Companies buy salesforce.com's SFA product because they believe it will give their business a competitive advantage—they'll be able to manage their pipeline better, make more effective decisions, compress sales cycles, increase sales productivity, drive collaboration, forecast better, centralize customer data, and use that data to develop more effective customer relationships. There's only one catch—the company is going to realize the value of its purchase only if its salespeople actually *use* it. This is where Loyalty 3.0 comes in. Studies have shown that the most important factor for success in any enterprise software deployment is gaining user buy-in and usage, much more so than the functionality of the software, organizational change management, or process alignment. Success factors are outlined graphically in Figure 7.2.

In particular, for SFA software (although we use the salesforce.com platform in this case study, the principles apply to any SFA product or implementation), you need your salespeople to

1. **Initially adopt the software.** It's much easier to do what you've always been doing than to learn something new.
2. **Use it on an ongoing basis.** If salespeople don't continue to use it, the company doesn't see any of the benefits.

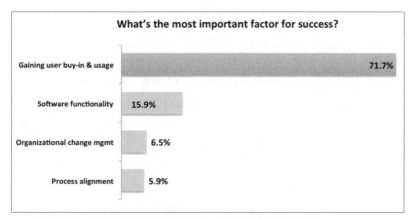

Figure 7.2 ENTERPRISE SOFTWARE SUCCESS FACTORS.
Source: Neochange, Sandhill Group, and Technology Services
Industry Association.

3. **Keep data quality high.** Data is the lifeblood of SFA sys-
    tems, and without good-quality data nobody will use the
    system, and the company won't derive any benefit.

    If you fail at any single one of these, your entire SFA sys-
tem will fail, and the cost of failure not only goes beyond what
you spent on the software, customization, and training, but it
also affects job satisfaction and perception of organizational fit
and can lead to increases in absenteeism and turnover.[8] Sounds
grim, no? But wait, it gets worse. Your salespeople aren't going
to voluntarily do the "right" things. They typically view SFA
systems as:

- Yet another system that IT rolls out that provides them with
  little benefit
- Data-entry work that takes time away from selling
- A loss of power through having to share contacts and
  knowledge
- A way for sales managers to micromanage them

- Something new that they have to learn
- Change (and change is hard)

There's a reason that some industry wags refer to SFA as "sales forced automation"—because salespeople need to be forced to use it! The giant elephant in the room of the enterprise software industry is the myth that if you deploy software to your employees, they will adopt it and effectively use it, maximizing the return on investment on your purchase. This myth conveniently ignores the fact that there are humans involved in the equation and that those humans might not be motivated to do the "right" thing. And this is the reason why analysts estimate that 50 percent of customer relationship management (CRM, of which SFA is a subset) deployments fail to meet expectations.[9] In this case, SFA systems clearly provide tremendous benefits, but the bulk of those benefits accrue to the company and management and not to the individuals doing all the work. So what typically follows after you deploy an SFA system is what we affectionately refer to as the *pain chain*:

1. The sales vice president mandates that salespeople have to use the SFA system: "If it's not in the system, it didn't happen."
2. Salespeople don't because they don't see the benefit. Data remains in spreadsheets or in people's heads.
3. The sales vice president spends a large percentage of his time hounding people to use the SFA system and issuing threats.
4. Salespeople have an even greater aversion to the system.
5. The sales vice president, realizing that it isn't working anyway, tells salespeople to enter as little data as possible and "just sell."

6. The pipeline is in disarray, customers are dissatisfied, and the company has no forecasting ability.

7. The sales vice president gets frustrated (or replaced). The company reinstates and/or revamps the system to collect an exhaustive amount of information.

8. Repeat the cycle.

Clearly, this is a people problem and not a technology one. What's needed is an automated, scalable way to motivate salespeople to want to adopt SFA systems, keep data quality high, and drive ongoing use. This sounds like a Loyalty 3.0 problem, doesn't it? Recognizing this opportunity, Bunchball built a Loyalty 3.0 application that integrates directly into salesforce.com's SFA platform, called Nitro for Salesforce (Figure 7.3). It consumes the user-activity data that salesforce.com generates as sales professionals are using it and uses that data to motivate "good" behavior. Salespeople earn points for closing deals, advancing opportunities, hitting their quota early, collaborating,

Figure 7.3 NITRO FOR SALESFORCE PROFILE PAGE.
Source: Bunchball, Inc.

maintaining good data quality, following approved sales processes, and any other behavior that the sales manager wants to drive. They can spend those points in a reward store for tangible or intangible rewards at the discretion of the sales manager. And as they hit various point thresholds, they level up and earn even more points as well as access to new goals.

Every salesperson is given a list of goals to accomplish (Figure 7.4), which can be a mix of:

- **Onboarding goals**, such as, "Add your *first* lead," to teach salespeople how to use the system
- **Evergreen goals**, such as, "Close a million dollars in business"
- **Time-based goals**, such as, "Win 10 opportunities *this quarter*"
- **Limited-availability goals**, such as, "Be *one of the first five salespeople* to close 10 deals worth more than $150,000 and hit 110 percent of your quota"
- **Personalized goals** assigned to salespeople based on their *specific attributes*, such as, "For field salespeople in the western region who have completed the Product X training, earn a reward when you sell 10 of Product X"

For any goal, the salesperson can track her progress at any point in time, see what she needs to do to complete it, and see how much time she has left. The salesperson also can see who else in the company has completed it, which serves a number of purposes:

1. There's a sense of life and activity in the program; you know that others are being active and accomplishing goals.
2. There's a competitive element because you want to catch up with and even surpass your peers.

Figure 7.4 NITRO FOR SALESFORCE GOALS (CHALLENGES) LIST.
Source: Bunchball , Inc.

3. If you're having difficulty with the goal, you know exactly whom you can go to for help—someone who has already achieved it.

This "real-time statistics dashboard" of progress lets salespeople know exactly how they're doing with respect to all the measurable goals their sales manager has given them.

Individual leaderboards are also available on any metric that the sales manager wants to drive (e.g., dollar leaders, quota leaders, most opportunities closed, etc.). Importantly, each leaderboard has a "Me" view and a "Top 10" view, as discussed in Chapter 4. If you have a sales team of 2,000 and a top 10 leaderboard, 1,990 people won't be very motivated and may in fact be demotivated, thinking that they'll never get on the leaderboard. The "Me" view always shows the salesperson in the middle of the leaderboard, even if he's in 1,000th place. So he'll see the four or five people above him and the four or five people below him, and he'll know exactly what he needs to do to move up a rung on the ladder and keep himself from falling down a rung. At the end of the day, we're really most concerned about our own performance, right?

To drive collaboration and competition, the sales manager has the ability to create one or more leagues and, within each league, any number of teams (Figure 7.5). A salesperson can be a member of one team in each league—for instance, he or she might be on the "West" team in the "Regions" league and the

Figure 7.5 NITRO FOR SALESFORCE TEAM STANDINGS.
Source: Bunchball , Inc.

"Financial Services" team in the "Verticals" league. Each league has a leaderboard showing how all the teams in the league are faring against each other. Teams also have collective goals to accomplish, such as "Close one million dollars in business by the end of the quarter." If the team reaches its goal, everyone on the team is rewarded. And there's competition within a team, with leaderboards showing who has contributed the most and the least to the team (Figure 7.6). Nobody wants to be the weakest link, the one who's not doing his part for the team.

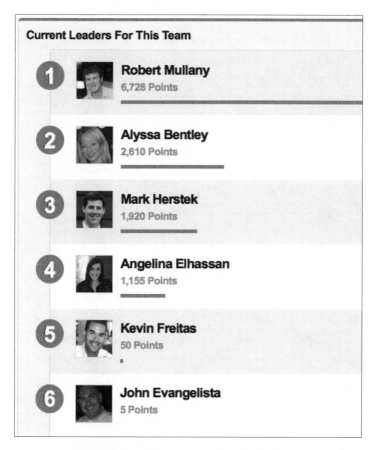

Figure 7.6 NITRO FOR SALESFORCE INTERNAL TEAM LEADERBOARD.
Source: Bunchball , Inc.

Microsoft Beta1

During the development of Windows Vista, Microsoft would send out e-mails asking for employee volunteers to test the latest in-development version. They didn't typically get a huge response. In an effort to increase the number of volunteers, the company built the Beta1 Game, in which employees earned letters for testing Vista. You earned a *b* for installing a beta, an *e* for voting on a version, a *t* for running it overnight, and so on until you earned the word *beta*. Then the company put up a page on the corporate intranet that showed everyone's name and his or her letters next to it, from the top contributors with *beta* down to the non-contributors with no letters. Just by making everyone's status in the game publicly visible, the company quadrupled participation in testing overnight. People were complaining when they didn't get letters that they felt they deserved and were bragging about their status on the leaderboards. Beta1 demonstrated not only the power of competition but also the power of community and social norms.

Finally, the sales manager can provide real-time feedback to salespeople as they interact with salesforce.com. Figure 7.7 shows that the user just earned five points for adding a new lead and that he immediately received a notification to positively reinforce that behavior. In addition, you'll notice that the application detected that the salesperson had filled out the bare minimum and so rewarded him with only five points but notified him that if he had filled out more data, he could have earned more. Instead of threats and mandates, which are typical in this scenario, the sales manager can use incentives to motivate good behavior.

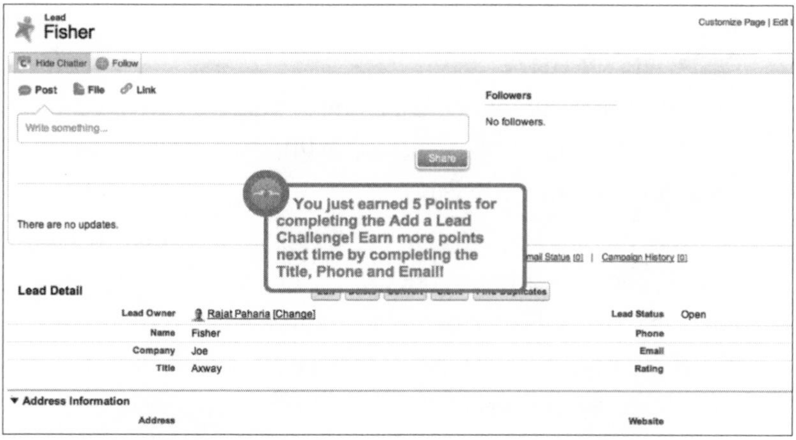

Figure 7.7 NITRO FOR SALESFORCE FAST FEEDBACK VIA NOTIFICATIONS.
Source: Bunchball , Inc.

By analyzing the user-activity data captured by Nitro for Salesforce, sales managers can begin to detect the key activities and behaviors that correlate with better sales performance and then use their "motivation engine" to drive more of those behaviors among weaker performers. This is a big contrast to traditional sales incentive programs, which are all about the result—"Hit 150 percent of quota, and you'll get a big bonus." Sales managers know from years of experience that there are everyday activities around process and data hygiene that lead to better sales results, but in the past they haven't had any way to efficiently track and reward those small, everyday behaviors. Now that the entire sales process is being executed online, sales managers can finally track and incentivize these "foundational" behaviors and reap the benefits. By addressing the "people problems" in their SFA deployments through Loyalty 3.0 principles, businesses can realize the benefits of their software purchase while at the same time driving peak performance from their sales professionals.

Customers for Life

One of the benefits of being a cloud software provider such as salesforce.com is that you have full visibility into customer usage patterns because all the software is running on your servers. By analyzing this big data, you can tell what features they're using and not using and when they encounter problems, and you can proactively advise customers and give them help. Salesforce.com has a dedicated team called *Customers for Life* (CFL) that is directly responsible for customer success and contract renewals. Given that salesforce.com is a subscription business, the company needs to re-earn its customers' business every year, so the role of the CFL team is critically important. Retaining existing customers costs much less than acquiring new ones. Part of the CFL team's methodology is to be constantly monitoring how its customers are using salesforce.com products and using predictive analytics to determine which customers are not adopting and seeing business value and are therefore at risk for attrition. This "Early Warning System" enables CFL representatives to proactively reach out to customers and help them better use their software, thereby ensuring a successful renewal when the contract term is up.

The CFL team doesn't keep this big data about software use and user activity itself. Team members also send the administrators at all their customers a monthly "Personalized Account Review," which includes a variety of metrics that shows administrators how their organization is using salesforce.com. This automated system gives the administrators the ability to act as their own early warning system (Figure 7.8), detect potential issues inside their own companies, and address them. Given that salesforce.com

Company Name

Usage snapshot for October 7, 2012 (9/2/2012 - 10/7/2012)
Last updated 15 days ago.

Company:	Company Name	**Account Team**		EWS
Org ID:	00D200000000GXR	**Success Resource:**	James Parker	CFL
Renewal Date:	June 2013	**Account Executive:**	Anthony Anderson	

Peer Group:				
Cloud:	Sales, Service (USG) & Custom	**Edition:**	UE	CFL
Industry:	High Tech	**Portal User:**	Yes	Inte
Account Type:	Standard			

Utilization Score: **1.9**

☐ Under Utilized   ☐ Data Storage   ☐ Process Management   ☐ Process Automation   ☐ Peer Group Median: ☐ C

TRUE LOGIN % (NON-PORTAL)
81%
Change: -9.05%
Peer Group Median: 74.03%

LICENSE UTILIZATION % (NON-
65%
Change: 49.77%
Peer Group Median: 91.60%

TRUE LOGIN % (PORTAL)
0%
Change: 0%
Peer Group Median: 18.01%

LICENSE UTILIZATION % (POR
0%
Change: 0%
Peer Group Median: 28.56%

CRUDS/USER (STANDARD OBJECTS)
165.16
Change: -19.70%
Peer Group Median: 124.96

RECORDS/USER (STANDARD OB
4545.30
Change: -22.35%
Peer Group Median: 4579.03

CRUDS/USER (CUSTOM OBJECTS)
7.78
Change: 41.03%
Peer Group Median: 32.48

RECORDS/USER (CUSTOM OBJE
255.26
Change: -20.18%
Peer Group Median: 6939.10

REPORT VIEWS (LAST 14 DAYS)
1.59
Change: -20.45%
Peer Group Median: 0.66

REPORTS/USER
20.65
Change: -22.46%
Peer Group Median: 6.78

Figure 7.8 SALESFORCE.COM'S EARLY WARNING SYSTEM DASHBOARD .
Source: Copyright© Salesforce.com, Inc. Used with permission.

has over 100,000 customers, it's crucial that the company leverage big data and automation to deliver customer success at scale.

- **Concept.** A sales-motivation program designed to engage sales teams and motivate them to adopt sales force automation tools, use them on an ongoing basis, and drive data quality

- **Business goals.** Competitive advantage from better sales insights and performance

- **Gamification mechanics.** Fast feedback, transparency, goals, badges, leveling up, onboarding, competition, collaboration, community, points

- **Big data.** User activity, sales performance, collaboration, quality measures, software use

- **Results.** Increased adoption and use of sales force automation tools, increased data quality, increased annual revenue, increased average deal size, increased lead closure rates, increased lead conversion rates, increased reps achieving quota, decreased average sales cycle, decreased rep time-to-productivity.[10]

Wrapping It Up

In this chapter we've seen how companies have integrated Loyalty 3.0 into work to motivate networking, social-media sharing, collaboration, sales, and overall job performance.

From here we jump into Part 3, "Direction," and look at how you can leverage everything you've learned so far to build your own successful Loyalty 3.0 program.

PART
3

DIRECTION

*If you don't know where you are going, you
might wind up someplace else.*

Yogi Berra

CHAPTER 8

Planning Your
Loyalty 3.0 Program

Whether you're Joe's Deli or a large multinational corporation, you can implement Loyalty 3.0 in your business and gain a competitive advantage in your market. Now that you understand how big data and motivation power gamification and have seen several examples of Loyalty 3.0 in action, you have the necessary foundation to build your own Loyalty 3.0 program. And although many of the examples that we reviewed in the preceding chapters were automated by technology, a tech-driven solution is by no means a requirement. In fact, you can implement Loyalty 3.0 in any of the following ways:

- With high- or low-tech tools
- With a big or small investment
- By yourself or with the help of a vendor or partner

All these paths are perfectly valid and, when done well, will lead to meaningful business results.

The Loyalty 3.0 Road Map

This chapter provides the framework—really a road map—for designing and implementing Loyalty 3.0 in *your* organization. The road map covers four essential steps, steps that will probably sound familiar to you if you've ever run a development project of any kind: plan, design, build, and optimize (Figure 8.1).

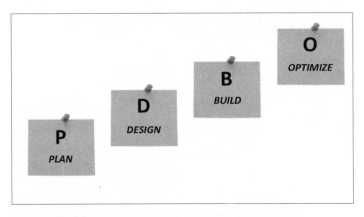

Figure 8.1 PLAN, DESIGN, BUILD, AND OPTIMIZE (PDBO): THE LOYALTY 3.0 ROAD MAP.

In this chapter we'll cover the planning step, and in Chapter 9 we'll cover the design, building, and optimizing steps. Regardless of the size and kind of business you're in, if you follow these four steps, you'll end up with a dynamic and engaging Loyalty 3.0 program.

Plan

As in any business initiative, the *plan* step lays the groundwork by identifying the problem and the proposed solution, figuring out the ROI, and getting buy-in from the rest of your organization so that you can move forward. This is a big step, so naturally it contains a few important steps of its own:

1. Identify the problem.
2. Identify your audience.
3. Identify the desired audience behaviors.
4. Establish your key performance indicators.
5. Create a mission statement.
6. Understand the playing field
7. Calculate the ROI.
8. Sell it to internal stakeholders.

Step 1: Identify the Problem (What Are You Trying to Do?)

What specific problem do you want to address? Loyalty 3.0 principles can have a positive impact on any number of business metrics—often several simultaneously. What are the pressing issues your team, division, or workforce is facing today? Do you need to motivate employees to perform better with respect to key metrics, like LiveOps? Engage a customer community to extend and enhance your products, like SolarWinds? Train customers on your complex product, like Adobe Photoshop? Or maybe you've identified that increased fan engagement, like Club Psych and MTV MegaFan, will be a key contributor to your future growth?

From 2001 to 2005 I worked for IDEO, an international design and innovation consultancy. While there, I learned several good aphorisms concerning the topic of design and innovation. One of my favorites was, "Do the right thing, and do the thing right." It's strategy and execution in a nicely wrapped turn of phrase and an implicit acknowledgment that both are equally important. If you don't have a clear idea of the problem that you're trying to solve, then it's impossible to "do the right thing."

Remember, a big part of "doing the right thing" is knowing what *not* to do. There's never a shortage of things that *can* be done, but you probably have a limit to the resources (i.e., time, money, and attention) that you can spend on this project, so the challenge at this stage is to determine where to focus—what's most important to your business *right now*?

Step 2: Identify Your Audience (Who Are Your Users?)

Now that you have identified the core problem or problems that you'd like to address, it's time to consider who exactly is involved. Your audience may be relatively broad, such as "fans of *Psych*." Or it may be more specific and narrow, such as "help-desk agents dealing with financial services customers." Understanding the *who*, the target, adds depth and richness to the problem you're trying to solve. This is why, after doing their initial user research, designers often will construct *personas*— archetypes of the various users they're trying to serve, with a name, picture, and complete backstory, so that as they're designing, they can constantly ask themselves, "What would Molly do in this situation? What would *she* think? What about Joseph? What would *he* do?" These personas enable Loyalty 3.0 designers to more viscerally inhabit a user's shoes, as we'll see when we get to the design phase.

Step 3: Identify the Desired Audience Behaviors (What Do You Want Your Audience to Do?)

What are the specific behavioral changes that you're trying to motivate that will solve the business problem you've identified? You've seen a number of different examples in the case studies, from exercising more, to contributing quality content, to buying more product, to sharing on the social networks. The only limiting factor here is that it needs to be something that you can track because, as we know, without data there is no Loyalty 3.0.

For example, if you want customers to visit your retail location more often and at off-peak hours, then you'll need a way of knowing when they're physically there and at what time. There are a number of ways you could implement this, ranging from low-tech and self-reported (customers add their names, date, and time to a signup sheet in the store) to high-tech and automated (an app running on the customer's phone automatically detects his presence in the store).

As in the problem-definition stage, specificity is key here. Rank order the importance of the various behaviors you want (we'll come back to this list in the design phase), and focus on the top of the list. Items on the list might include:

- Visit our retail location more often.
- Visit our retail location at off-peak hours.
- Register.
- Get better customer-satisfaction ratings.
- Close more high-value deals.
- Spend more.
- Add more items to their cart.
- Spend less time on support.
- Create more quality content.
- Share more to social media, etc.

Step 4: Establish Your Key Performance Indicators (How Are You Going to Measure Success?)

At this point you understand the problems that you're trying to solve, who your audience is, and what the desired behavior change is. Now you need to figure out how to measure whether your Loyalty 3.0 program is having any impact on your problems. The statistics that you choose to measure and monitor, which bridge the gap between user activity and business value, are your key performance indicators (KPIs). They enable you to determine your progress in relation to your goals, see the change in your program performance over time, and assess whether or not your program is a success. KPIs can be many and varied and will vary widely from industry to industry, but the key factor is that they will always be measurable. Examples of KPIs from our case studies might include:

- Number of users registering for the program
- Average customer-satisfaction score
- Average call time
- Number of social-media shares
- Number of page views on a website
- Number of questions answered
- Number of documents shared
- Number of users creating content
- Number of likes and shares of content
- Average order value
- Average number of items in cart
- Time spent on support
- Number of leads entered
- Number of training lessons completed per user
- And many other possibilities

Step 5: Create a Mission Statement (What Is the Program Goal?)

With the information you've generated, create a *mission statement* that clearly articulates the desired business results and the role that Loyalty 3.0 will play in helping you to reach your specific goal.

As an example, suppose that the issue you want to address is an underperforming partner program. The audience is your company's partners. The behaviors you'd like to influence are partner focus and sales activities. The desired result is an 18 percent increase in partner channel sales. Therefore, your mission statement would read, "Our Loyalty 3.0 partner program will keep resellers more focused on our brand, extend sales efforts on our behalf, and increase our partner channel sales by 18 percent." Where did the 18 percent number come from? It's either aligned with bigger business goals ("We need at least an 18 percent increase in partner channel sales to hit our number this quarter") or is just an informed, reasonable target at which to aim. In either case, you need to put a stake in the ground to give your team a measurable goal to work toward and to be able to determine whether your program was successful or not.

Here are some additional examples:

- "Our Loyalty 3.0 program will drive the individual members of our sales team to fully use our CRM solution an average of twice per week."

- "The Loyalty 3.0 program on our website will engage our customers, promote loyalty, and increase our customer retention rate by 36 percent."

- "Our Loyalty 3.0 program will encourage our customers to buy more sandwiches, share our weekly offers with their friends, and contribute new sandwich ideas to us, leading to a 15 percent increase in revenue."

- "Applying Loyalty 3.0 principles to our marketing team will instill a sense of competition, drive productivity, promote company loyalty, and reduce our attrition rate by 20 percent."

If you can't articulate a clear mission statement, then it's back to the drawing board with you! Once you have it on paper, read it again and make sure that it fits into your overall business strategy. Still good? Congratulations, you now have a North Star to start sailing toward, not to mention an elevator pitch to use with your colleagues!

Can You Use Loyalty 3.0 Everywhere?

There's a reason that none of the case studies we looked at included standard corporate websites. These sites are typically "brochure-ware"—a catalog of static pages with no opportunities for users to interact or participate. This lack of interaction makes these poor candidates for Loyalty 3.0 programs because:

- There's nothing a user typically can do, except look at pages.

- These sites aren't typically designed for repeat visits—they're meant to be consumed once. Long-term engagement isn't the goal.

- There is no existing relationship between the site owner and the visitor, so the site owner has little to no insight into what motivational techniques will work.

The following reflect the key points that you should keep in mind as you're working through your Loyalty 3.0 project:

- The nature of the core experience that you're working with

- The quantity and frequency of interaction it supports
- The duration of the engagement that you're looking for
- The value you can provide to participants for engaging with you

Anyone can implement Loyalty 3.0 into an experience where the goal is loyalty, engagement, or an ongoing relationship, but not every experience has that goal. It might just be that your core experience doesn't lend itself to Loyalty 3.0. That said, as we witnessed in the Foursquare case study, Loyalty 3.0 principles can drive meaningful short-term engagement around simple (or nearly nonexistent) interaction. Just don't expect to retain those users for the long run.

Step 6: Understand the Playing Field (What Are the Boundaries?)

Here's another good adage I picked up at IDEO: "Builders think better." What does this mean? If you've never built a can opener and someone asks you to design the best can opener you could possibly think of, it probably would cut with a laser, be remote-controlled via Bluetooth, and would clean itself. Sounds awesome, no? Because you don't have direct experience of the real-world constraints (e.g., cost, manufacturing, materials, electronics, the laws of physics), you don't know what you don't know, and you design something that isn't feasible or even possible.

If you gave someone who had experience building can openers the same task, her experience and knowledge of the possible would inform her design, and you'd end up with something realistic. This is not to say that the experienced builder is any less creative. Experienced builders are creative within the boundaries of the possible, boundaries that come only from firsthand knowledge and experience. Research has shown, in fact, that constraints paradoxically serve to increase creativity rather than decrease it.[1]

Before you jump into the design phase of your Loyalty 3.0 program, you should understand the constraints you're working within. What data do you need to power your program, how are you going to get it, at what granularity, and how often? What resources do you have on hand (time, money, people) for initial implementation and then ongoing maintenance? If there's a technology component to your solution, what functionality does it provide you? Does it enable you to create teams, personalized goals, and progressive disclosure? How easy or hard is it to administer, and will people need special training to do so? What kind of data, reports, and insights are you going to get out of the system, and in what ways will your company be able to consume and act on it?

Build or Buy?

If you're using a high-tech solution, this is the time to determine whether you intend to build it or buy it. You want to make this decision at this stage for three reasons. First and most important, you need to know the constraints before you jump into the design phase. If your technology platform (built or bought) doesn't support certain functionality, such as team goals, you need to know that now because it's going to set the boundaries that you need to work within. Second, your vendor or partner can provide you with an experienced point of view on ROI and strategy so that you don't have to reinvent the wheel. Finally, when constructing your ROI model and crafting a pitch to sell Loyalty 3.0 internally, you can include the implementation plan or partner and the corresponding costs as a concrete part of it.

There are pros and cons to buying it or building it yourself depending on your budget, time frame, available tech resources, scale, and other factors. You might want to build it yourself if:

- Your solution is low tech.

- You have internal development resources available.

- You have internal resources with loyalty, motivation, engagement, and gamification experience.

- No data of any kind can leave your premises (because most vendors run in the cloud).

- You are creating a very simple implementation that won't change and doesn't need to be administered or evolved over time.

- No vendor has a specific piece of functionality that is critical to your program.

- Your solution will be used by a small number of people.

The advantages to working with a specialized vendor (such as Bunchball) include:

- Expertise, experience, and best practices from working with a wide range of customers across a range of industries

- A proven process for getting from concept to launch

- Scalable, secure technology

- Decreased time to market

- No development risk

- A completely outsourced solution, enabling you to focus on your core competency

- Future-proofing—platforms that are continuously enhanced, eliminating the risk of obsolescence

- Easy-to-use administration, localization, reporting, and analytics tools requiring little to no involvement from your information technology (IT) team

- Networks of partners who can provide other services: design, development, reward fulfillment

- Existing integrations into popular platforms, such as Salesforce, Jive, Drupal, Magento, IBM Connections, and so on

- Mobile capabilities already built in

- Existing customer communities that enable you to learn and share best practices

Step 7: Calculate the ROI (How Do I Justify This?)

Now we get to the place where the rubber meets the road—the *return on investment*. It's important to start thinking about ROI at this stage, even though it seems early. Return on investment—a financial, dollars-and-cents return, a *positive* one—is necessary not only to secure any organizational buy-in and investment but also to make sure that your Loyalty 3.0 strategies and tactics align with your business objectives.

It's easy to forget about ROI as we think of those really nice things we'd all like to have as an organization—lots of customers, loyal customers, and lots of interaction with those customers. As we found out during the dot-com bubble, though, we can invest, invest, and keep on investing without ever making any money. As with any other initiative your business might pursue, implementing Loyalty 3.0 requires a solid business case.

ROI should be top of mind or near top of mind throughout the Loyalty 3.0 exercise—through the planning stages, initial implementation, and ongoing fine-tuning and optimization. There are two principal stages where ROI needs to be on the front burner. One is now, when organizational buy-in and strategic alignment are important to secure. The second stage starts once you've launched—to measure *ongoing* ROI. Collected data and metrics determine "reality versus plan" and are used to optimize your program so that you can ensure positive ROI throughout its lifetime.

The ROI calculation involves figuring out how much you think you're going to spend and how much you think you're going to make. Because you haven't actually built it yet, calculating your spend is going to involve some estimating. Working with an experienced partner or vendor can help here because that partner can give you a pretty accurate assessment of upfront and ongoing costs. If you're going to build it yourself, then you'll need to put together rough estimates on:

- Cost to develop/implement any technology you might need (including hardware costs)
- Amount of ongoing people hours and costs needed to maintain and run the program
- Cost of any rewards offered

Obviously, if you're implementing your system on a whiteboard in your local car dealership, your costs will be pretty low—lower than a Loyalty 3.0 program for 300,000 sales representatives around the world using a completely automated system. Most implementations fall somewhere in between.

Your return, or how much you're going to make, is a function of the dollar value of your KPIs combined with the impact of your Loyalty 3.0 program against those KPIs. Sometimes your KPIs directly correspond to revenue—if users add extra items to their shopping cart, you'll see a corresponding increase in revenue. Easy! Most of the time, life isn't so simple. How does a customer sharing your content more affect your revenue? An employee collaborating more? Increasing customer-satisfaction ratings? These don't always have direct revenue ties, but we all know that these things are valuable and indirectly drive the top line. In these cases, your KPIs act as proxies for dollars, and the challenge is to figure out the dollar value of each. To do this, you will need to leverage industry standards and benchmarks, along with the experience of other team members, to develop assumptions and model the financial impact of each KPI.

For estimating the impact of your program, you already took a stab at that when you created your mission statement. If you're working with an experienced vendor or partner, that partner probably can share the results that others have seen in a similar context. Even if you're going it alone, it's valuable to visit vendor websites because they often publicize their customers' results. And, of course, there are the case studies in this book as well as supplementary information available at the Loyalty 3.0 website: www.loyalty30.com. Using information from the sources described here and any other information you have at your disposal, give the goal in your mission statement a reality check and make sure that it still seems achievable.

At the end of the day, there should be a positive ROI. If there isn't, something is wrong somewhere within your Loyalty 3.0 case.

Keep Them Coming Back for More: Decreasing Employee Attrition Levels as an ROI Example

Suppose that your Loyalty 3.0 program's goal is to decrease employee attrition levels by 20 percent over the next year by increasing employee engagement. You do a little fact-finding. According to the Society for Human Resource Management, it costs about 38 percent of an employee's annual earnings to replace him, which includes training and recruitment, costs associated with the separation process, and productivity losses owing to workflow disruption. Additional studies by Chartcourse estimate that it costs $40,000, on average, to replace a nurse, whereas technology companies can run up replacement costs of more than $125,000 per vacancy.

Suppose that your human resources department conservatively estimates the cost of replacing employees at your technology company to be approximately $40,000. If your company has 1,000 employees and a 5 percent annual attrition rate, 50 people will voluntarily depart in the next 12 months at a cost of $2 million to the business. Reducing the churn rate by 20 percent therefore will save the company $400,000 in the next year alone.

That's a great start to illustrating an ROI, but it doesn't stop there. You also should consider the side effects of raising your company's employee engagement level. Engaged employees are more profitable employees, more productive employees, and they add more value more quickly. These characteristics are hard to place a value on but should be considered when calculating the potential value of greater employee engagement.

Step 8: Sell It to Internal Stakeholders (How Do I Get Organizational Buy-In?)

Once you build the ROI and its related assumptions into a business case, the next step (unless you're Joe of Joe's Deli fame and make all the decisions yourself) is to sell it to the rest of your organization. Loyalty 3.0 programs often will touch many parts of a company and may require active sponsorship from a variety of organizational units. Depending on the size of your company, this may involve building a team of executive sponsors and peer promoters, securing budget, and bringing in your tech team for scoping, due diligence, and technical governance. The end goal is to get buy-in and investment from senior management and all stakeholders—anyone affected by the program.

You'll want to present the business case to these stakeholders—the concept, the goals, the strategy, and the ROI at a minimum. Because people grasp concepts better through stories, you also can share the case studies in this book, or relevant others that you may find, to tangibly illustrate to your peers and managers how Loyalty 3.0 can have a meaningful impact on your business.

Step One of Four: Completed!

You've run the gauntlet, attained buy-in from the powers that be, and are now ready to get down to business. Well done! You've already laid the groundwork. Next comes the fun part: creating your Loyalty 3.0 experience.

Planning Loyalty 3.0

- The four implementation steps are plan, design, build, and optimize.
- Planning consists of the following activities:

- o Identify the problem.
- o Identify your audience.
- o Identify the desired audience behaviors.
- o Establish your key performance indicators.
- o Create a mission statement.
- o Understand the playing field.
- o Calculate the return on investment.
- o Sell it to internal stakeholders.

- Vendors and partners cannot only supply the nuts and bolts for Loyalty 3.0, but they also can help with strategic planning, ROI analysis, and experience design.

- Remember, your program isn't Loyalty 3.0 if it isn't collecting and using data to create a better experience with a higher return for your organization.

CHAPTER 9

Bringing Your Loyalty 3.0 Program to Life

You've planned, you've modeled, you've sold, and now you're ready to stop talking and start doing. So let's dive right in!

Design

People often ask me if we have game designers on staff at my company, Bunchball. My answer is always an emphatic "No!" because Loyalty 3.0 is not a game-design problem. Game designers make games—experiences created from scratch with the singular goal of entertaining—and Loyalty 3.0 programs are not games. If anyone tries to sell you a game designer to design your Loyalty 3.0 program, you should run away screaming.

What kind of problem is it, then? It's an *interaction design* problem. As defined by Wikipedia, *interaction design* is:

> [T]he practice of designing interactive digital products, environments, systems, and services. Like many other design fields, interaction design also has an interest in form, but its main focus is on behavior. . . . Interaction design is heavily focused on satisfying

*the needs and desires of the people who will use the
product."[1]*

Don't let the word *digital* throw you off—you can use interaction design in low-tech scenarios just as easily as in high-tech
scenarios. So how are we going to use interaction design to create our Loyalty 3.0 program? There are three main steps:

1. Understand your users.

2. Decide what you want them to do.

3. Design the experience.

Step 1: Understand What Motivates Your Users

World-renowned design and innovation firm IDEO promotes
"human-centered design" as one of its central design tenets. As
the name implies, human-centered design starts with a keen
understanding of the human in the equation and how humans relate to and interact with products, services, technology,
brands, businesses, and so on. The work you did to identify your
audience in the planning phase was a good start; now you get to
build on it. The first thing you should do, to quote Steve Blank,
a serial entrepreneur and academic, is "get out of the building"[2]
and talk to the humans you want to engage with your program.

There are various levels of fidelity of "getting out of the
building." The highest is actually getting out of the building
and talking to your users in the context where they interact with
your product. Companies such as Intuit have famously been
doing this for years, with its "Follow Me Home" practice.[3] In
Intuit's early years, company founder Scott Cook would hang
out at a local Staples store, wait for someone to buy Quicken,
and then ask to follow the customer home so that he could
observe how the product was installed and used. The goal was
not to interfere or assist, just to observe and learn. And by be-

ing in context with the customer at home, Cook was able to experience the situation exactly as the customer did, with all the distractions, technology glitches, and paperwork that real people experience. Cook then would take that learning back to his teams to make the Quicken experience better.

At lower fidelities, you can interact with your users over the phone or via e-mail, instant messaging, or message boards. These experiences aren't as rich as personal visits, but they're more scalable (especially if you're dealing with a distributed or global audience) and are generally less time-consuming.

This isn't the time for selling your program and your vision; it's to learn about why your users are engaged (or disengaged!) with your business in the first place and what motivates them. Whether they're customers, partners, or employees, have a friendly, informal conversation, and ask a lot of "Why?" questions. Even if you think you already know the answer, it pays to approach these discussions with a "beginner's mind" because you can always learn something new.

We all tend to think that we know what motivates and drives other people, but we're not always right. We have a tendency to envision our users as one-dimensional, only caring about the part of their life that interacts with our business and uses our product or service, which is probably why we call them *users*. In reality, along with being our users, they're people, with rich, deep lives that affect and color how they interact with us.

For example, consider a LiveOps contact-center agent. A mental image, however fuzzy, will appear in your head. Imagine trying to design a motivation system for that agent. As an "outsider," you might have some rough ideas and some preconceived notions, but you really don't know what drives these particular distributed contact-center agents. If you work at LiveOps, depending on your level of interaction with the agents, your picture could be considerably sharper, and you may have enough insight already, just by putting yourself in an agent's shoes, to create a compelling experience. Even then, you can still benefit from having a conversation with your users with the context of your program in mind. Read these quotes from actual LiveOps agents:

> *"LiveOps has been a great way for me to become a dedicated business owner. Through LiveOps, I have learned many skills on how not only to understand the customers but to make the sale. They provide you with skill and knowledge to question through the awesome courses they offer. LiveOps is a huge part of my life, and I would not change that for anything. LiveOps is number one!"*

> *"LiveOps is the greatest company to work for. I am 65 and unable to handle a full-time job. I have worked for corporate America since I was 15 years old. I have finally found a company to work for that makes life so much easier. I use my customer-service skills to make people have a wonderful phone experience. The beauty of this job is that I can work from home, name my own hours, ask for help, and receive it when needed and do not have to put on my makeup. Thanks LiveOps."*

> *"I joined LiveOps in 10/2005. I was so excited to find something I could do from home. I had been through surgeries for spinal injuries and was told I would never work again. I am a prime example that is not so. I have been blessed to work with a group of people who care and help you to advance and learn the virtual environment. I worked in a call center prior to my in-*

juries. However, I never enjoyed my work as much as I do now with the variety of calls and customers. I am so thrilled with my choice to remain with LiveOps over the years. I did leave LiveOps for a few months due to family health and soon learned when I went to work for another at-home company. It was not Live-Ops and did not give me the satisfaction I found with LiveOps. So LiveOps I will always be here to supply my services as long as I am needed."[4]

All of a sudden you're seeing in 3-D. Physical disabilities limiting opportunities, aging out of the traditional workforce, autonomy, flexibility, training and skill development, receiving help, community, the desire to want to make people happy—all these jump out at you and can inform the design of your Loyalty 3.0 program. You now know what motivates your workers, what they value in their jobs, and how important their peers are, and you can now integrate that knowledge into your design. And all you had to do was ask.

You don't even need to talk to very many people. Usability consultant Jakob Nielsen has shown that to get the best results from usability tests, you don't need to talk to more than five users.[5] From my experience doing user research at IDEO and from building Loyalty 3.0 programs since 2007, I've found that the same value curve applies to user research for Loyalty 3.0 programs (Figure 9.1).

As Nielsen states on his website, useit.com, "The most striking truth of the curve is that *zero users give zero insights*." Once you've talked to one user, you're already getting valuable insights. By the second user you're hearing some things you've heard before. Beyond the second user, you increasingly hear the same things from each subsequent user so that by the time you reach the sixth user, you're learning very little that's new.

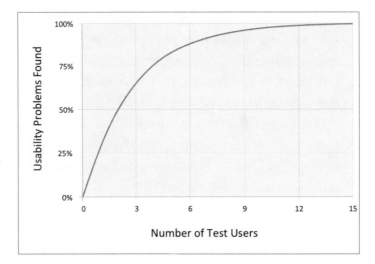

Figure 9.1 HOW MANY USERS DO YOU NEED TO TALK TO IN ORDER TO FIND MOST OF YOUR PROBLEMS?
Source: (useit.com.)

One thing to note: If you happen to have very different user groups that you're trying to engage with the same program, then consider talking to at least three people in each group.

Once you've talked to a few humans, it helps to aggregate what you've learned into personas, as we discussed in the "Identify Your Audience" section in Chapter 8. Personas are valuable for a number of reasons:

- They help you segment your users into archetypes that may have different motivations.
- They make your users real instead of abstract.
- They give you a lens through which to look at every design decision.
- They provide a shared language for everyone on your team. You can say, "Molly wouldn't do that," and everyone immediately knows what you mean. Because, like you, they know Molly.

- They're the stars of the scenarios you'll develop when you're designing the user experience.

Finally, if you're implementing Loyalty 3.0 inside a community, you also should understand the nature of that community. Some communities lend themselves very well to competition, such as sales communities. For others, competition is completely inappropriate, and collaboration is valued instead. Every community has an inherent nature, and your Loyalty 3.0 program needs to align with that nature in order to be successful.

Step 2: Decide on the Key Activities You Want Your Users to Do

From your initial planning work, you're already 75 percent of the way there on this one. In the *plan* phase, you created a ranked list of the behavior changes that will positively affect your KPIs. Pull that list back out, and for each item on the list, you need to create a corresponding *action* that can be tracked. For instance, on the list in Chapter 8 we had the example behavior "Spend more." The trackable action in our program, the thing that the end user actually does, would be "Checked out," and it would be triggered whenever the user paid for the items in her cart. Along with the action, we also would want to capture the dollar value of the cart because that's the metric we're trying to drive. We'll call this extra data that goes along with the action *metadata* (data about data). Here's how we can use this action and metadata with some of our gamification mechanics:

- **Goals.** Give the user a goal, such as, "Check out with more than $100 worth of items in your cart."
- **Badges.** Award the user with a badge the first time he checks out with more than $100 worth of items in his cart.

- **Fast feedback.** When the user earns the badge, show her an instant notification congratulating her and letting her know what the next achievable goal is.

- **Collaboration.** Users can be part of a team representing their local school. When the team's aggregate purchases reach $10,000, the school earns a reward.

- **Points.** Users can earn one point per dollar spent, to be redeemed on discounts or rewards.

Similarly, the "Add more items to their cart" behavior from Chapter 8 would use the same "Checked out" action because it would be triggered by the same event. In this case, we'd add metadata that indicated how many items were in the cart, and if we're tracking transactions over time and keeping a running total of the number of items purchased, we can create a goal such as, "Buy more than 30 items from our store this year."

The "Close more high-value deals" behavior would work very similarly to the "Spend more" behavior. There would be an action named "Closed a deal" that would be triggered whenever a new contract was signed, and the metadata would be the size of the deal. So we could create a goal such as, "Close 10 deals worth more than $150,000 this quarter."

The "Get better customer-satisfaction ratings" behavior would require an action named "Completed customer-satisfaction survey" that would be triggered every time a customer completed a survey. The metadata would be the customer's overall satisfaction score, as well as the name or ID of the agent who serviced the customer. In this case, we'd now be able to create a goal for a help-desk agent such as, "Get five good customer-satisfaction ratings in a row."

The "Share more to social media" behavior might have several corresponding actions. There could be one for sharing to

Facebook, one for sharing to Twitter, one for sharing via e-mail, and so on. Corresponding goals could be "Share five articles by e-mail" or "Share 25 articles via Facebook, Twitter, or e-mail."

By now you get the idea. This step is about translating your desired user behaviors (the ones that drive your KPIs) into discrete, trackable actions and metadata, which are the building blocks on which you build your goals. You now have the foundation that you need to build your Loyalty 3.0 program.

Now that we have the tracking pieces in place—the specific things your users are going to do that you care about—it's time to create goals for your users around those actions, such as the examples we gave earlier. Here are a few sample goals for a sales team—a mix of goals that are achievable only once, as well as some that can be accomplished over and over:

- Close 10 deals worth more than $150,000.
- Enter 10 full contact records for C-level executives.
- Hit 100 percent of quota in the first six weeks of the quarter.
- Advance an opportunity.
- Share a story of a new customer win.
- Complete Product X training.
- Sell your first Product X.
- Team goal: Close $5 million in new business in your region.

Your list length will vary depending on the size and complexity of your implementation, and you should have a rough sense of the value of each of these goals because they're derived from the ranked lists of user behaviors and actions that drive your KPIs. Once you have this list of goals, you need to figure out how you're going to reward users for accomplishing each goal, and if you're awarding points of any kind, how many. Find the goal on the list that you think has the lowest value, and give that one a score of "1." That's your baseline unit—nothing the user does (that you care about) will be worth less than that, only more. Now go through the rest of your list, and score everything else relative to your baseline unit.

As an example, suppose that you decide that a user "advancing an opportunity" (moving a prospect a stage forward in the sales cycle) is your baseline unit. It's indicative of forward progress as well as properly following an established sales process, so it's worth tracking and rewarding. The next action on your list is for the user to "share a story of a new customer win." This requires more engagement on the part of the user. Instead of a single click, the user has to conceive of and write something—and she's sharing an experience that is likely to be of value to the entire sales community. Is that worth twice as much as advancing an opportunity? Five times as much? You make the call based on how much you value that behavior.

At this point you should also determine whether the participant should earn a badge for achieving this goal. The questions to ask yourself are: Is the accomplishment notable enough to deserve a badge? And is this something that a participant would be proud to share with her colleagues? At the end of this process, you'll have a table that looks something like Table 9.1.

We can use this list as the basis for a point system. A straight 1:1 translation would mean that the user would earn 1 point for advancing an opportunity, 8 points for sharing a story of a new customer win, and 60 points for completing Product X training. Or scale all the numbers by 100, and the user will earn 100 points for a advancing an opportunity, 800 points for sharing a customer win, and so on. The important thing that you did was to determine the relative value of these goals to each other, and from there you can use any scaling factor that you like. As a best practice for scaling factor, think about the scale of numbers that

Goal	Relative Value	Badge
Close 10 deals worth more than $150,000	200x	Yes
Hit 100% of quota in the first 6 weeks of the quarter	150x	Yes
Team goal: Close $5 million in new business in your region	150x	Yes
Sell your first Product X	100x	Yes
Complete Product X training	60x	Yes
Enter 10 full contact records for C-level executives	30x	No
Share a story of a new customer win	8x	No
Advance an opportunity	1x	No

Table 9.1 RANKED GOALS AND THEIR RELATIVE VALUES

people find interesting with respect to their local currency. So in the United States, hundreds and thousands are good scaling factors—not too small as to be "not worth it" and not too big as to devalue the points.

Imagine that your sales team is using the reward structure just discussed. Upper management suddenly decides that Product X is extremely important to the company and that selling it is a top priority, more so than anything else. Remember our discussion about steering wheels and accelerators from Chapter 4? It's a simple matter to go into your Loyalty 3.0 program and reprioritize Product X training and sales and add new goals around selling more of Product X, to turn on a dime and refocus your sales team.

With this ranked list of goals, we now have two lenses through which to evaluate our Loyalty 3.0 program as we work through a design. The first one is the user lens that we created through our personas. Now we also have the business lens, as reflected in the key behaviors and activities that we're trying to motivate and their relative worth to the business.

Step 3: Design an Experience that Motivates Users to Do These Things

Here's where we "tell a story" about a compelling Loyalty 3.0 experience that engages the user and accomplishes the business objectives. With the story in hand, we can then flesh it out into a spec that our development team can follow.

Tell a Story

Crafting a compelling Loyalty 3.0 experience is a design problem, and like all design problems, there is no "right" answer. What we do know is this: If we look at the experience through the users and business lenses and it rings true, it's probably good. So our very first step should be to write a story, or scenario, about our personas interacting with our product or service.

Walk through your existing experience, and at each key interaction point, ask yourself if there is some Loyalty 3.0 principle or gamification mechanic that could be used to motivate the persona to take a desired action, and write it into the story.

Make sure that the interaction rings true and doesn't feel forced or unrealistic. Put yourself in the persona's shoes, and ask yourself the questions: "Would Molly really care about that? Would she really make the effort to engage here?" If the answer is "No," then take it out. This isn't about adding things to the experience for the heck of it; it's about meaningfully enhancing the experience and motivating your users. This is your chance to be creative, within the constraints of what's enabled by your technology, what motivates your users, and what satisfies your business objectives.

Don't Forget Your Tools!

As a refresher, recall the 10 gamification mechanics from Chapter 4, which we present again in Figure 9.2. And keep in mind how this set of gamification mechanics was used effectively in the case studies in Part 2.

Fast Feedback	*I get immediate feedback or response to actions.*
Transparency	*I can see where everyone (including me) stands, quickly and easily.*
Goals	*I have short-and long-term goals to achieve.*
Badges	*I can display evidence of my accomplishments.*
Leveling Up	*I can achieve status within my community.*
Onboarding	*I can learn in an engaging, compelling way.*
Competition	*I can see how I'm doing against others.*
Collaboration	*I can work with others to accomplish goals.*
Community	*I can see what the community is doing; the community can see me.*
Points	*I can see tangible, measurable evidence of my accomplishments.*

Figure 9.2 THE 10 GAMIFICATION MECHANICS.

Run your story by your team, look at it through the lenses of your personas and the business, and then finally, run it by some of your users and see what they think. Does it ring true to them? Incorporate their feedback, and iterate until you've addressed all the major issues, always keeping in mind the famous Voltaire quote, "Perfect is the enemy of good."[6] When you're done (when it's good), you'll have a compelling story that you can share with anyone in your company and a guideline for your development team to use as it builds the experience. You're one step closer to that North Star!

Sample Scenario

Check out the Appendix for an in-depth Loyalty 3.0 sample scenario about engaging attendees of a tech company's annual conference. Go ahead and read it now. We'll wait.

Ten Tips from the Expert's Playbook

We've been doing this a long time, across hundreds of customers and many different industries. While you're creating your scenario, here are 10 key things that you should think about.

1. Think with Arcs

People need beginnings and endings; otherwise, experiences turn into endless grinds with no sense of closure. Certain experiences have built-in *arcs*, like LevelUp for Photoshop, where there are 12 missions, and when you're done, you're done. This is a *content arc*, where the limited quantity of content creates a natural arc for you. Long-term engagement isn't the desired outcome here; you're after short-term engagement that gets users to the end.

For long-term, ongoing, sustained engagement, you need to use *time arcs*. Most experiences have some sort of natural time arc to them—a TV show has a season, a company has a fiscal quarter, and so on. And if there are no natural arcs, then make one up—a day, a week, a month, a quarter, or a year, whatever is appropriate for your context. All the goals that you give users then should reflect that time frame—"Invite 10 friends this month," or, "Close 20 deals this quarter." This gives users a deadline and acts as a forcing function on activity and a chance to start anew if they didn't hit their goals during the current time period. The experience "resets" every time period, and everyone has a new chance to excel.

Frequent-flyer programs, because most people don't fly that often, use a one-year time arc—you have a year to accrue enough miles to level up to the next tier. If you don't make it, you can try again the following year but are forced to start over at zero. While completely appropriate for a frequent-flyer program, a one-year time arc wouldn't work in a call center, where people need more immediate feedback and have short-term goals—there you'd want to use a day, a week, or on the outside, a month as the time arc.

2. Put Levels and Goals on a Curve

Next, consider how you want your users to level up. When spacing out your levels, consider making the first few achievable in a fast, easy progression. This is a great way to get users engaged quickly and feel a sense of accomplishment and progress. After they're engaged in the program and have a good set of accomplishments under their belts, space the levels out farther to make them harder to achieve. When plotted out on a graph, the levels should map to an exponential curve, as shown in Figure 9.3. This isn't new; levels in the workplace and in the military follow this same general pattern—promotions are relatively quick early on in your career because you're at the bottom of the ladder, but once you reach a certain level, it takes a lot more work and effort to move up to the next tier.

The same rule applies for goals. Early goals should be relatively easy, and as the user gains skill and experience, the goals should get progressively more difficult. When awarding badges for goal completion, one powerful technique to use is to create a set of badges that includes several easier goals combined with one or two more difficult ones. Participants will accomplish the

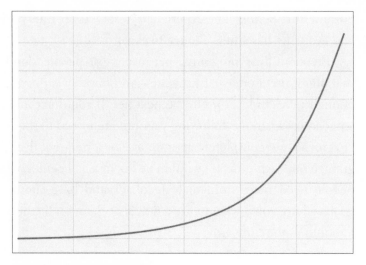

Figure 9.3 THE GOAL CURVE.

easy goals, but then in order to collect all the badges and complete the set, they'll need to take on the more difficult tasks.

There are two other concepts worth mentioning here:

- **The endowed-progress effect.** Riley and Jake both go to the car wash, where they get loyalty cards that are stamped every time they come in for a wash. Riley's card has eight empty slots, and when he fills them up, he gets a free car wash. Jake's card, on the other hand, has 10 empty slots, but the first two are already filled in with "free" stamps. So the end result is the same: They both need to get eight car washes in order to earn a free one. Do you think there will be any difference in how many car washes Riley and Jake each get?

    It turns out that Jake will be more likely to fill up the card, and he'll do it faster than Riley. Jake's card has reframed his task as one that has been undertaken and incomplete instead of one that hasn't yet begun, and that's enough to increase Jake's commitment level to the task.

This is one of the reasons for making initial levels and goals easy to accomplish—they are effectively "free stamps" that increase your participants' commitment to their goals.

- **The goal-gradient effect.** Research has shown that people who are closer to a goal exert more effort toward that goal and that this extra exertion increases with proximity to the goal. In Jake's case, he was relatively closer to his goal, 20 percent of the way there as opposed to Riley's 0 percent, and therefore, he put more effort into reaching his goal, which in this case meant getting car washes on a more frequent basis and filling up his card faster. You'll notice this in your Loyalty 3.0 program—as your users get closer to the next level or accomplishing a goal, their level of activity will increase. This is why it's important to have a mix of short- and long-term, easy and hard goals to accomplish so that users are always in close proximity to a goal.

3. Keep It Fresh

As part of your design planning, think about how you're going to introduce new elements into your program over time to keep it interesting. Some experiences have the benefit of a constant supply of new, engaging content (such as TV show sites) that the Loyalty 3.0 program can extend to cover. Others don't, so they need to introduce new "campaigns" over time, along with the time arcs described earlier, to keep things interesting. These can include short-term individual and team goals, which optionally can be driven around real-world events (e.g., "The March Madness Challenge") as well as limited-availability rewards.

4. Use Progressive Disclosure and Personalization (Segmentation)

You'll notice in the scenario in the Appendix that Laura saw only one mission at the beginning—to add her profile photo.

Once she did that, she unlocked a whole new set of missions personalized to her based on her answers to the registration questions. There might be thousands of goals in the system, but she saw only one "out of the box" and then six new ones that were directly relevant to her once she had completed the first one. This showcases two key concepts:

- **Prerequisites.** Goals can be sequenced and shown only when certain prerequisites are met. By doing this, at any point in time the user is only seeing what's relevant to him right now and is not being distracted by goals that aren't relevant at this point in his life cycle.

- **Personalized (segmented) goals.** Take advantage of what you know about users—personal attributes, historical data, earned entitlements, and so on—to provide appropriate goals for them. By doing this, you can set the right goals for the right people at the right time and not distract them with irrelevant information.

5. Enable Participants to Share Their Accomplishments

Enabling your users to broadcast their achievements to sites such as Facebook and Twitter is a great way for them to share their accomplishments with their social groups while at the same time generating interest and traffic to your program. Adobe and USA Network both used this strategy to expand the reach of their customer programs, and as we saw in Bluewolf's case, you can also use Loyalty 3.0 principles to motivate your employees to push the company's marketing message through their megaphones.

6. Deliver Surprise and Delight

People love to be surprised by good things. Leverage that in your design, and provide them with surprise and delight moments that keep them hooked and wanting more. The best way to do do this is with badges, where the two key mechanisms are:

- Mystery badges that users know they can earn, but they don't know what they need to do to get them.

- Surprise badges that users don't know that they can earn but that appear once they've been earned.

Both of these create an *information gap* that people's brains treat like catnip. What do I have to do to earn the Mystery Badge? What did I do to earn the Surprise Badge? Your users will be connecting with each other on your forums and at the company water cooler frantically trying to figure out the answers to these questions.

7. Be (Slightly) Unpredictable

Along with information gaps, the other thing that people's brains like is an element of randomness and variability in rewards. People get accustomed to things quickly, and then they become the *new normal*. There are two good ways to prevent this from happening, and they can be used individually or in combination.

- **Variability in the reward (aka "mystery box").** In this case, participants are working toward an unknown reward—it could be small, it could be big, but they won't find out until they earn it.

- **Variability in the reward frequency.** If you're planning on rewarding participants for every n times they do something (e.g., "100 points for every 10 deals closed"), then you can add an element of variability here to keep them on their toes. Sometimes they'll need to close only 7 deals to get the reward; other times they'll need to close 13.

They'll never know if the next reward is right around the corner, and this will motivate them to close that one more deal.

8. Beware of Unintended Consequences

The biggest problem that we see in people's initial foray into Loyalty 3.0 systems is misaligned incentives. If you're running a community site and the goal is to drive traffic, do you want to be motivating and rewarding people for posting? If you do, you're going to get a bunch of garbage posts in your forums as people abuse the system for rewards. You didn't really want a large quantity of meaningless posts—while your post metrics have gone up, overall, you're damaging the community. What you really want to reward is quality posts.

So how do you determine quality without having IBM's Watson supercomputer at your disposal to analyze the content of every post? You enable your users to rate or "like" each other's posts, and then you reward a user only when one of her posts is rated highly or liked. Perhaps you even charge users some of their virtual currency to make a post in the first place so that they'll only do it if they're confident enough that they'll make the currency back from the community "bestowing" positive ratings on the post.

In a contact center, if compensation is tied to shorter calls, you can expect agents to rush customers off the line. If compensation is tied to customer satisfaction, you can expect agents to transfer angry callers to other agents so that they don't get penalized and have their pay reduced. The rules of the system are undermining your intent, so you need to think carefully about how to design your program so that you actually get the behavior you desire.

You may not get this right the first time, and that's okay. You can rest assured that your users, ever helpful, will help you to find any misaligned incentives.

9. Gaming the System

Along those same lines, your users also will help you to find any loopholes in your system. Are you rewarding a user with points every time he makes a status update? Then don't be surprised when someone writes a script that updates his status every second. Where there's a will, there's a way! On the one hand, the user's "cheating" damages confidence in the entire system, so you need to address it quickly and decisively. On the other hand, you definitely know that your users are engaged. To prevent this problem in the first place, put automated controls on any repeatable reward, such as, "Can be earned only twice a day," or, "Can't be earned more frequently than once every two hours," so that you're still driving the desired behavior but only at the desired frequency.

10. Enable Peer Recognition

Loyalty 3.0 programs don't have to be completely about a system or set of rules determining rewards. You also can add a social element to your program by enabling your users to give to each other. Users can give each other points, badges, virtual items, or anything else that carries value in your program. And the motives for giving can be anything from kudos for a job well done, to wanting to get to know someone, to just being altruistic and generous. Referring back to our discussion on reputation, when used in the workplace, this is another *bestowed* element that can complement what we know about the employee and give us a more well-rounded picture of her contribution and performance in our program. At the same time, it's yet another way to satisfy our desire for social interaction.

Where's the Fun?

You'll notice in this book that I have rarely, if ever, mentioned *fun*. And that's because Loyalty 3.0 is about motivation, not about fun. Can fun motivate? Absolutely. Do I know how to create fun? No. Fun is one of those very abstract, fuzzy notions that can't really be captured, quantified, and defined. If I'm playing *Call of Duty*, and I get shot and killed, am I having fun? If I'm playing in a tennis match, am I having fun? If I'm trying to solve a puzzle for hours, am I having fun? The answer to all these questions is, "It depends." What it depends on has nothing to do with the task itself and everything to do with my motivation for wanting to do these things, which brings us back to our core motivators. If my parents are forcing me to play tennis and I don't want to (I have no autonomy), then I'm not having fun. If I'm playing of my own free will, enjoying the challenge, and feeling like I'm getting better, then I am. So when you're designing your Loyalty 3.0 program, forget about fun, and focus on *motivation*.

Step Two of Four: Completed!

You've created a compelling story that demonstrates Loyalty 3.0 principles integrated into your experience, and you've figured out how to motivate your users while at the same time solving your business problems. You, my friend, put the "uperstar" in *superstar*.

Build

Whether you're building the whole thing yourself or integrating with a vendor's platform, now it's time to start making things:

creating specs, starting implementation, and making sure that you're setting the stage for success.

Spec It Out

Your scenario provides the bones, but now you need to put enough meat on them that your development team can actually build your Loyalty 3.0 program. This is typically done with a product specification document largely consisting of user flow diagrams and wireframes, tools that are used for the design of any kind of interactive experience.

User flow diagrams describe how users navigate through the experience and are typically built using standard flowcharting tools. Each stage in the user flow corresponds to a wireframe that illustrates the user experience at that stage (Figure 9.4).

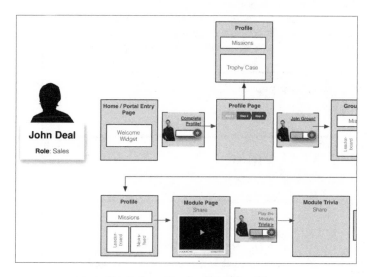

Figure 9.4 SAMPLE USER FLOW.

Wireframes are a series of schematic storyboards that focus on:

- The kinds of information displayed
- The range of functions available

- The relative priorities of the information and functions
- The rules for displaying certain kinds of information
- The effect of different scenarios on the display[7]

Figure 9.5 shows a sample wireframe from a mobile application.

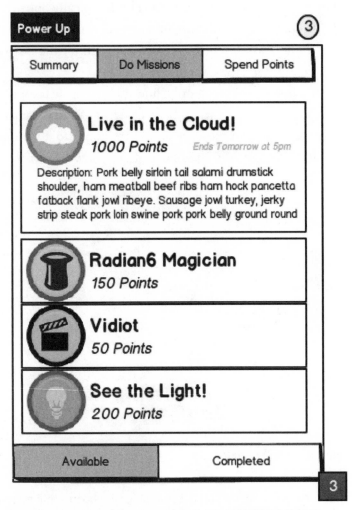

Figure 9.5 WIREFRAME FOR A MOBILE APPLICATION SCREEN.

Between the scenario, user flows, and wireframes, you now have clear documentation of your design intent. While you might not have all the specific details worked out, you have enough to get started and fill in the gaps as you go along. Once you have these done and in a format that your product team can use, you're ready to start building! If your team follows an agile development methodology, then the scenario will be the source of the user stories that you feed the development team. Each user story can have corresponding flows and wireframes.

The actual technical details of implementation are a bit beyond our scope here because they will vary according to your existing systems and the goals you're trying to achieve. But here are some things to keep in mind as you roll your program out.

Use the Key Integration Points

Typical digital Loyalty 3.0 implementations have four key integration points:

1. User activity data needs to be pushed out of the core experience and into the Loyalty 3.0 engine. Ideally, this data is being delivered in real time as users are interacting with the system so that the system can provide fast feedback and instantly updated statistics.

2. Loyalty 3.0 user-experience elements should be embedded into the core experience. As we saw in the case studies, businesses need a way to display Loyalty 3.0 elements to users in order to motivate them. The typical pattern here is to have a small, persistent element that is always present, such as the sidebar on Nitro for Salesforce, combined with dedicated pages to which a participant has to explicitly navigate that contain more in-depth information.

3. Notifications are the typical way that Loyalty 3.0 systems provide fast feedback and should be embedded throughout the experience so that as users are accomplishing goals, they are receiving immediate positive reinforcement.

4. If the experience has some sort of news feed or status wall, Loyalty 3.0 systems can post user achievements to that feed or wall in order to spread the word about the user's accomplishments in the community.

In addition, in order to keep each user's statistics separate and distinct, every participant must have a unique user ID that is used when interfacing with the Loyalty 3.0 program. This is typically the ID that the user uses to log in to the system or the system's internal ID for the user.

Place the Hooks

As you're building, make sure that you have the hooks and feeds in place to capture all the data that you need to track your KPIs and clearly prove the success of your Loyalty 3.0 program. It's important to do this now so that you don't find yourself, three months after launch, unable to tell if your program is a success or not.

In addition, if you're using any of the other big-data techniques outlined in Chapter 3 (e.g., cluster analysis, machine learning, microsegmentation, etc.), make sure that you're capturing the relevant data and storing it in a format appropriate for further analysis.

Establish Baselines and Control Groups

There are two main ways that businesses demonstrate the efficacy of their Loyalty 3.0 programs:

- **Before and after.** The business knows how it was doing against its KPIs before, and it can see how it's doing against its KPIs after implementing the Loyalty 3.0 program. Assuming that no other changes have been made, this change can be attributed to the program. Note that this requires "before" data. If you don't have this data prior to the build of your Loyalty 3.0 program, then you can run your program in *silent mode* for a period of time. Silent mode means that all the user-data activity is being captured, but none of the motivation mechanics are being shown to users—their experience doesn't change at all, but you're now capturing KPI data to establish a baseline to measure against. Once you're satisfied that you have enough data, you can activate the Loyalty 3.0 program for users and measure how it changes their behavior.

- **Control groups.** Some businesses have the flexibility to be able to have a *control group*, a subset of users that is running in silent mode, as described earlier (see "A/B Testing" in Chapter 3). Then the business can compare the KPIs for the group that was exposed to the Loyalty 3.0 program versus the group that wasn't. Adobe, for instance, was able to compare the KPIs from Photoshop users who had experienced LevelUp against those who hadn't.

Decide at the outset which of these your implementation can support, and make sure that you have the necessary infrastructure to enable it. For instance, if you're using treatment and control groups, you will need a way to determine who is in each group (in a way that eliminates any potential biases), and to measure each group's results separately.

Communicate the Program—Inside and Out

Good programs have good communications. Before launch, make sure to explain to internal stakeholders what will happen, when, what the measures will be, and what the impact will be. When you launch your Loyalty 3.0 program to your users, make sure to communicate it to them via all appropriate channels. As part of your program content, include a "Getting Started" guide that explains the program to users, and if there are new processes or products that need to be learned, take a lesson from LevelUp for Photoshop and include that onboarding process in your program. As you enhance the program and roll out new features over time, continue to communicate those to your users. Otherwise, like the experienced Photoshop users who missed new functionality, your users won't know and won't engage.

Step Three of Four: Completed!

You built it, and they came. People are being motivated by your Loyalty 3.0 program, and your business is seeing results. There's talk around the office that you might be the next CEO. But it's not time to rest on your laurels just yet!

Optimize

Your Loyalty 3.0 program, fueled by user activity, is generating lots of data. This data on its own can give you insights into what's working in your program and your overall experience and what isn't, and when used in conjunction with data from other systems (e.g., web analytics, customer relationship management, sales force automation, etc.) can be used to see how your program is affecting larger business goals. There are a number of ways to analyze and visualize this big data, several of which we described in Chapter 3, ranging from simple graphs and charts in Excel to complex visualizations from tools such as Tableau and languages such as R.

Here is a small sampler of the types of reports you can generate from Loyalty 3.0 data.

Cohort Analysis

Cohort analysis, covered in Chapter 3, can be used with any of the KPIs that you're trying to drive. In the example in Figure 9.6, the leftmost column shows how many new users joined the program in the indicated month, each of which is a cohort. The columns labeled "1" through "12" indicate how many of the users from that cohort returned in each subsequent month for the following year.

Month	New Users	Returning Users											
	0	1	2	3	4	5	6	7	8	9	10	11	12
March	13,269	5,004	4,241	4,270	3,953	3,723	3,656	4,116	3,696	3,499	3,267	3,365	2,467
April	5,004	3,655	3,440	3,211	3,057	3,006	3,099	2,868	2,788	2,577	2,555	2,071	
May	3,655	3,065	2,855	2,761	2,683	2,645	2,482	2,441	2,272	2,227	1,877		
June	3,065	2,673	2,573	2,492	2,428	2,311	2,231	2,103	2,077	1,771			
July	2,673	2,429	2,358	2,266	2,166	2,088	1,995	1,969	1,699				
August	2,429	2,253	2,163	2,070	1,996	1,910	1,879	1,641					
September	2,253	2,120	2,020	1,945	1,856	1,820	1,607						
October	2,120	1,976	1,901	1,817	1,793	1,584							
November	1,976	1,846	1,769	1,742	1,553								
December													
January													
February													

Figure 9.6 COHORT ANALYSIS.

Pareto Analysis (The 80:20 Rule)

Pareto analysis enables you to recognize your most engaged participants and their behavioral profiles (Figure 9.7). This information can be used to target specific groups of users as well as help to recognize the key activities that drive your participants to an engaged state.

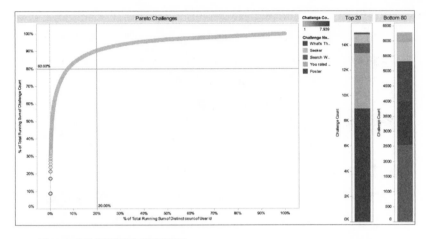

Figure 9.7 PARETO ANALYSIS.

Time-Stamp Analysis

Time-stamp analysis provides you with insight about *when* users are interacting with your program (Figure 9.8).

Figure 9.8 TIME-STAMP ANALYSIS.

Drop-off Analysis

Create a funnel of any kind, whether it's a sequential set of actions you want a user to take, a set of levels that you want a user to progress through, or a set of pages that you want the user to navigate in a particular order. With that in hand, you can do a drop-off analysis to see where you're losing users and redesign and optimize accordingly (Figure 9.9).

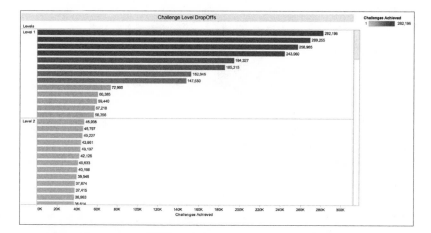

Figure 9.9 DROP-OFF ANALYSIS.

Dashboards

For everyday use, what you really want is something that you can look at once a day and, with a single glance, get a sense of the health of your program. This is where dashboards come in—you can use your Loyalty 3.0 program data to create a single dashboard page that has your most important KPIs on it (Figure 9.10). Ideally, it gets sent automatically to you every day so that there's zero friction in your being always up to date. And if something catches your eye or an early-warning system that you've set up triggers an alarm, such as salesforce.com's Customers for Life group has, you can drill in to get more details.

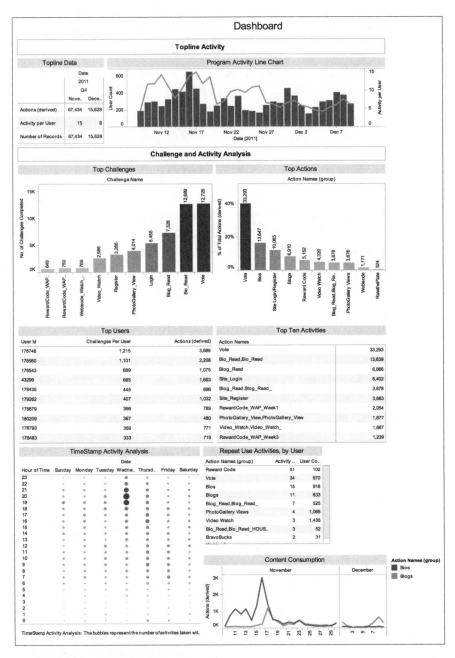

Figure 9.10 KPI DASHBOARD.

Once you have the details, because you're working with people and motivation instead of product, you now have the ability to react, modify, and iterate on the fly. Whether you're reprioritizing goals, driving traffic to new parts of an experience, or reacting to a real-world event, not only can you see what's going on, but you also can act on it.

At the end of the day, the key in any of these analyses is to make the data actionable so that you can use it to continuously iterate and refine your program, always with the goal at the end of the day of driving your KPIs and maximizing your ROI.

Step Four of Four: Completed!

You have dashboards and reports that enable you to keep your finger on the pulse of your program. But you also have a steering wheel and gas pedal that you can use to change user behavior in your experience at any point in time. Whereas in the past you'd see data and then be stuck in a six-month product cycle to try to do something about it, now you can respond in minutes. You're in the driver's seat. Welcome to Loyalty 3.0.

Designing, Building, and Optimizing Loyalty 3.0

- Design starts with an intimate understanding of what motivates your users. Developing user personas can help.

- Design continues with creating experiences that motivate behaviors and especially high-priority behaviors. Create a story, and then make a spec around that story.

- Build in the hooks you need to make sure that you're getting good data out of your program.

- Use the big data coming out of your program to continually optimize it and drive higher ROI.

- You now have the ability to respond to data and change user behavior in real time.

CHAPTER 10

Forward in All Directions!

Where We've Been

Congratulations if you've made it this far—it's been quite a ride!

- We started with a look at the current state of loyalty and how it's not actually working to generate any of the kind of loyalty that businesses really want.

- We examined the macro trends that are forcing businesses to redefine how they engage with their customers, employees, and partners.

- We learned about human motivation and identified five key intrinsic motivators.

- We took a tour of the big data landscape and explored the different ways that it can be used to drive business results.

- We learned about gamification, the Loyalty 3.0 engine fueled by motivation and big data, that uses intrinsic and extrinsic motivators to drive business value.

- We explored case studies about Loyalty 3.0 programs across consumer engagement, learning and skill development, and employee motivation.

- We finished up with a road map for how to implement a successful Loyalty 3.0 program.

At this point, you're armed and dangerous. You have the knowledge, the experiences of others, and the tools to evangelize and sell Loyalty 3.0 inside your organization, design a compelling program, and drive meaningful business results. Now let's turn an eye to the future.

Where We're Going

The Loyalty 3.0 industry is growing rapidly as more businesses and industries discover the power of big data, motivation, and gamification and apply it to their business problems. Aside from the industries that we've already seen adopting Loyalty 3.0 principles, in the next few years we're going to see industries including health care, retail, education, financial services, telecommunications, manufacturing, hospitality, energy, government, pharmaceuticals, medical devices, and insurance using Loyalty 3.0 to motivate and engage their customers, partners, and employees.

As Loyalty 3.0 continues to evolve, we'll also see the following.

Loyalty 3.0 Inside

Several of the case studies that we looked at—including Adobe's LevelUp for Photoshop and Nitro for Salesforce—involved a business embedding Loyalty 3.0 into the actual products it sells to its customers. We're going to see more of this, especially in businesses that have complex products and where customers are paying a subscription fee and can defect with low switching costs. This is most readily apparent in the software industry, where cloud-based software as a service (SaaS) is taking over from the old on-premise model of buying the software outright and deploying it on your own infrastructure. This shift to SaaS means that if a customer isn't deriving value, he can turn off a vendor's products in an instant. It's therefore imperative that the software vendor drive initial adoption and ongoing use in order to retain customers, guarantee renewals, and enable upsell opportunities.

For companies with free trials (such as Adobe) or a "freemium"-to-premium business model, Loyalty 3.0 can onboard users quickly, giving them the sense of mastery and the confidence necessary to convert from a free to a paid user and drive top-line revenue for the business.

Loyalty 3.0 Centers of Excellence

Big companies seeking to use Loyalty 3.0 principles will develop centralized teams that are the internal Loyalty 3.0 experts. These internal experts will provide services, support, and technology to the rest of the company, much like internal technology and social-media experts do today. By establishing these centers of excellence, companies will be acknowledging the importance of motivation, engagement, and loyalty to their businesses. By taking advantage of their broad view across the enterprise, these central teams will be able to create programs that span business units as well as internal and external constituents and leverage their breadth of experience to create great Loyalty 3.0 experiences.

The Loyalty 3.0 Federation

As more systems integrate Loyalty 3.0 principles, both participants and businesses are going to see the value in tying the systems together so that users have a single multifaceted "reputation." We've seen some companies in the consumer space do this with their own properties, such as Warner Bros. across the various movie sites and USA Network across its various TV show sites. Users can have a reputation for each show and an overall reputation as well.

In the workplace, you'll see this concept spanning different functional systems—sales-force automation, learning management systems, and social collaboration. Within each of these, there will be reputation in certain areas of expertise, such as "product management," "compliance," and "social media." The more systems that join the federation, the more detailed and rich the profile of each individual employee becomes. This profile, the employee "baseball card," provides the foundation for the workforce analytics vision outlined in Chapter 3, which I predict will be a massive opportunity area for Loyalty 3.0.

Loyalty 3.0 = Good Design

In a couple of years, Loyalty 3.0 is going to be called *good design*, and it's going to be a critical part of any business owner's toolkit. The macro trends that we identified are forcing business change, and case studies such as the ones we reviewed in this book have demonstrated that Loyalty 3.0 concepts and principles clearly work to motivate and engage participants.

The Loyalty 3.0 canon will continue to grow, with the latest research in behavioral economics, consumer psychology, marketing, and design feeding our understanding of how to create experiences that are not only compelling but also motivating. Interaction designers will make *motivational design* a key part of their design repertoire, and their purview will expand to include the *design of work*—taking the same design processes that are currently used to craft engaging consumer experiences and applying them to the entire employee experience at work.

Loyalty 3.0 is going to be table stakes for any business competing in the global marketplace because consumers, employees, and partners are going to expect and demand it as an integral part of their experiences. Businesses that don't understand and implement Loyalty 3.0 programs, that don't have a strategic initiative to drive engagement, motivation, and loyalty, are going to be left behind.

Wrapping It Up (Figure 10.1)

Figure 10.1 THE LOYALTY 3.0 EQUATION.

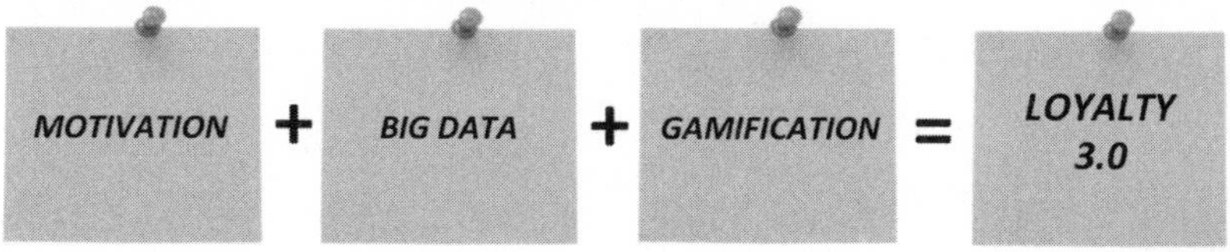

MOTIVATION **+** BIG DATA **+** GAMIFICATION **=** LOYALTY 3.0

Today's loyalty programs are like the Bruce Willis character in the movie *The Sixth Sense*—they're dead, but they just don't know it yet. They have failed at creating actual loyalty, at generating any competitive advantage, at keeping up with a rapidly changing world, and at engaging all the constituents that matter—a company's customers, partners, and employees. It's time to take back the word *loyalty* and make it actually mean something. By using the big data generated by our constituents as they interact with us, combining it with an understanding of human motivation, and using the data-driven motivational techniques of gamification, we now have the power to motivate, to engage, and to create true loyalty—Loyalty 3.0.

APPENDIX

A Loyalty 3.0 Sample Scenario: Engaging Attendees of a Tech Company's Annual Conference

In this appendix we take a quick look at the business requirements that a large tech company has concerning its annual conference. We follow that with a scenario that details the user experience before, during, and after the conference as a participant engages with a Loyalty 3.0 program. And we end with a short discussion of some of the key design drivers for the program.

While the following scenario is presented only as text, when you are working on your scenarios, you always should include rough sketches or wireframes of any user-interface elements to help people visualize the user experience and make it more tangible. At this stage it's important that the wireframes be intentionally rough so that they convey very clearly that they are mock-ups and not meant to be final screens so that people focus on the concepts rather than on any specific detail of the execution. Hand-drawn wireframes are great, and you also can use rapid wireframing tools such as Balsamiq Mockups that enable you to work on a computer but create mock-ups that look like sketches.

For more sample scenarios and mock-ups, visit the Loyalty 3.0 website at www.loyalty30.com.

Aperture Software: ApCon 2015 Business Requirements

With six venues, 500+ sessions, 36,000 attendees, and hundreds of partners, ApCon has become *big*. This presents the following challenges:

- Making all the attendees feel like they are part of a single ApCon community
- Finding common interests with other attendees when
  - Attendees have a wide variety of job roles.
  - Attendees use a wide variety of Aperture products.
  - Attendees have varying amounts of ApCon experience.
- Helping attendees (with all the varying characteristics above) understand how to get the most out of their ApCon experience
- Compelling attendees to participate—before, during, and after the live event
- Providing value to partners with higher-quality leads and incentives to drive traffic
- Keeping attendees focused on positives, not negatives
- Encouraging attendees to diversify in order to reduce crowding and overselling sessions
- Educating attendees on Aperture, partners, and solutions
- Leveraging the collective power of the ApCon community for good
- Collecting data on the actual, measured behavior exhibited by attendees so that Aperture can optimize the ApCon experience next year

Meet Laura

Laura was recently assigned to the Aperture Software development team at her company, Umbrella Corporation. Her manager suggested that she attend ApCon 2015 to learn the latest about Aperture Software technologies. She's never been to ApCon before but has heard from some of her colleagues that it's big, busy, and a lot of fun, so she's excited. She goes to the ApCon website and registers. As part of the process, she answers several questions, including questions about whether she's been to ApCon before, what her job role is, and what products she uses. She answers

- Never been to ApCon
- Job role: Developer
- Products used: Portal 2.0, Propulsion Gel, Light Bridges

Immediately after, she receives an e-mail in her inbox titled, "Welcome to ApCon 2015 and The Power of 10." What's that about? She opens the e-mail:

> *Greetings Laura!*
> *Welcome to ApCon 2015 and the Power of 10! In this 10th year of ApCon we want to do something special, something meaningful, something that leverages the power of the Aperture community to do good for the world.*
> *So here's the deal—there are 10 teams, and you're on the* Red Team, *led by our Chief Customer Officer, Gordon Freeman. You and the other members of your team earn Aperture Points (APs) for completing missions—before, during, and even after ApCon. You can see your mission list here—it's*

tailored specifically to you, based on your answers to our registration questions—and includes things like networking with others, signing up for sessions in advance, contributing to discussions, answering questions during sessions at ApCon, and more.

If your team can earn 1 million Aperture Points before the end of ApCon 2015, you'll unlock a $10,000 grant for the Grant-A-Wish Foundation. And if your team earns 1 million Aperture Points and is one of the top three teams, you'll unlock another bonus grant for the foundation.

Click here to see your first set of missions and here to connect with your team. And remember—the foundation is counting on you!

Best regards,
Team Aperture

Here's what Laura is thinking after receiving the welcome e-mail:

- This is not just another conference. I'm not just going to show up, listen to some people talk, and then leave.

- It's clear what I should do next. I need to go look at my missions and start doing them and connect with my team.

- I'm going to be contributing to this conference, not just a passive observer.

- I'm going to be actively involved not just during the conference but before and after as well.

- I'm part of a social unit, my team, so I have an immediate connection with my teammates and an obligation to them.

- I have an "us versus them" competitive feeling with the other teams.

- The goal of attending conferences is often to network, but conferences don't do anything to facilitate that. By making me part of a team with missions to accomplish, it facilitates my networking.

- By attending this conference, I'm going to do good for the world (not something I'd typically expect as part of a conference), and I feel accountability to the Grant-A-Wish Foundation—its success is in my hands.

- I like the connection to someone important at Aperture (an exec) who cares.

Initial Missions

Laura clicks on the link to see her missions and is taken to the ApCon 2015 website. She sees several tabs on the page, including Home, Profile, Team Standings, Teams, and Rewards. She's on the Profile page, and she sees her name, a placeholder for her picture, her team name, and a mission list. Right now there's only one mission showing in her list, the "Photo Booth" mission, which is to add her profile photo. It says she'll earn 10 points for doing so. She clicks on the link and uploads a profile photo. A little piece of "toast" pops up from the bottom of the screen and tells her that she's completed the "Photo Booth" mission and earned 10 points for her team and that she's unlocked new missions. That feels good!

As she's clicking back to her "Power of 10" profile, she notices that her point meter in the sidebar and on her Profile page have moved up and that she now has 10 points. She mouses over the "10 points," and it tells her that she has 490 more to go to get to level 2. Interesting—that shouldn't be very difficult.

She also notices that something has been added automatically to her status wall—a message telling everyone that she completed the "Photo Booth" mission. So whenever she completes a mission, everyone will know. That's cool! When she looks at her mission list again, she now sees that the "Photo Booth" mission is marked as complete, and a new set of missions has appeared. They are

- **Newbie.** Go watch the "Welcome to ApCon" video and pass a short quiz.
- **The Hacker Way.** Go to the session list and join at least one developer-oriented session.
- **Portal 2.0. — Hot Off the Presses:** Check out the latest Portal 2 news and pass a short quiz.
- **Propulsion Gel Mentor.** Share your favorite Propulsion Gel tip in the Propulsion Gel forums.
- **Advanced Light Bridges Webinar.** Attend the upcoming webinar to learn about advanced Light Bridges functionality.
- **Introduce Yourself:** Go to your Team Page and introduce yourself in your team's private forum.

Laura notices that the missions are clearly tailored to her, based on how she answered the questions during registration — it knows that she's new to ApCon and that she's a developer, and it shows only products that she uses.

Her Team

Laura clicks on the Red Team's name on her profile and is taken to the Red Team's page. She can see that the Red Team is currently in sixth place (Uh oh! Better get moving) and that the team currently has 60,754 points — quite a way to go to unlock the foundation grant, but there are still months until ApCon. Other things she sees on the Team page are Gordon Freeman's picture and a short message from him, team missions that the whole team needs to work together to accomplish, a private team forum where the team can discuss strategy, and a leaderboard showing who has contributed the most to the team. She's not on the leaderboard yet but can see that she can get on it with a little effort.

She reads through several of the introductions that others have posted to the group forum, and then she adds her own and completes another mission.

After spending some time on her Team page, Laura clicks through the other tabs. On the Home page is a news stream with the latest news from the ApCon team—updates, showcases of certain individuals, details on new missions, and rewards. And on the Team Standings page she can see all 10 teams and how they're doing in relation to each other.

Then she lands on the Rewards page—this looks like a store, with a bunch of items in a catalog, with pictures, descriptions, and prices. She can see her current point balance at the top, and items that she can afford have a highlighted "Buy Now" button. Things in the store include guaranteed seating at the Keynotes (she'd heard those were hard to get into), a meet and greet cocktail hour with the Aperture executive team, special box seats for the big concert, VIP tickets to some of the Aperture partners' parties, and more. There are limited quantities of most of the really good stuff, so she'll need to earn (and spend) fast. Laura likes that her points not only help out her team but also can help her get access to some special experiences as well.

Learning by Doing

Laura starts working her way through the missions, and as she completes them, more new ones appear. Some are for products that she doesn't use (such as GLaDOS and Turrets), but the missions for those products are to watch videos and read data sheets about the products, so by the time she's done, she knows about the entire Aperture product line.

There are also missions concerning several Aperture partners, and by completing them, Laura learns about new products and services in the Aperture ecosystem that she didn't even know existed. She makes a mental note to stop by the Black Mesa booth when she gets to San Francisco and is confident that she can have a good conversation because she's now an educated consumer.

Other missions are around forum activity on the ApCon site, spreading the word about ApCon via Facebook and Twitter, networking with other first-time attendees via the forums, and more. There are several developer-specific missions as well, including coding projects for nonprofits, submitting code recipes, and more.

As she's using the interactive agenda, Laura notices that each one has a point number assigned to it. Signing up for and then checking in at that session at ApCon earns you points! The interesting thing is that sessions that are already filling up have lower point values than others that still have lots of seats available. That's clever—they're using the points to encourage people to try new things and evenly distribute attendees.

As Laura is working her way through the missions, she's learning a lot, meeting new people (whom she can't wait to meet in person at ApCon), and earning points for her team and moving them ever closer to their million Aperture Point goal.

A month before ApCon, Laura receives the following message from Gordon Freeman:

Hello Red Team—
   We're four weeks away from ApCon, and we're in fourth place. Cave is starting to make fun of me

in our executive meetings, so we need to step it up! :)
Let's see if we can hit 1 million Aperture Points and
unlock the $10,000 grant for the Aperture Founda-
tion before ApCon; then we can focus all our energy
while there on being in the top three. The #1 team
gets bragging rights for the whole year, as well as
access to an exclusive special event at ApCon, and I
want us to be that team!

Click here to visit your missions list and start
earning more points. Every little bit counts, and
your teammates need you.

Get moving—time is running out!
Sincerely,
Gordon

Laura likes that Gordon Freeman is involved and reaching out
to her and the rest of her team directly and that he sounds like
a real human. It shows to her that Aperture is treating this seri-
ously and that the senior management there cares about what
happens.

Preconference

As ApCon approaches, new missions appear that prepare Laura
for the actual event. One of them is to download the AC15
mobile app onto her smart phone. Once she's done that, she's
given a series of missions to do via the mobile app, including
navigating through all the content and scanning a barcode and
QR code. She's never done that before, and it's very cool that
you can point your phone at a code and something happens!

Another new mission is called "I am a ____"—you have to
fill in the blank with something interesting about yourself, so
Laura says, "huge fan of the Chicago Bears. New to Aperture

development and loving it!"

And then there's the "Ask Me" mission, where she has to put in three questions that people should ask her when they meet her at ApCon and four answers for each, one of which should be correct. She's asked to put in one question about her job, one question about her work with Aperture, and one about her personal life, so she puts in

- "Ask me about the coolest thing I worked on at Umbrella Corporation."
  - o <Three wrong answers>
  - o Right answer: "The orange box."
- "Ask me about the biggest function I ever wrote."
  - o <Three wrong answers>
  - o Right answer: "1,000 lines."
- "Ask me: Team Jacob or Team Edward?"
  - o <Three wrong answers>
  - o Right answer: "Neither, Team Harry Potter!"

In the mission description for this mission and the "I Am A" mission, Laura reads that these will show up (along with her answers to the registration questions, such as products used, etc.) whenever someone else at ApCon scans her badge with his phone. The person will then have to ask her one or more of her questions and put in the right answer in order to earn points. She thinks that this sounds like fun—once again, Aperture is facilitating her networking and giving her a reason and a context in which to meet new people and talk to them.

Laura at ApCon

Laura's been excited all month, and now she's finally in San

Francisco for ApCon 2015. And the strange thing is, it doesn't feel alien and strange and like she doesn't belong, like most conferences do. She's been part of this community for months now, and the missions have prepared her for *everything*. She already has her schedule set, knows where and when she's going to grab lunch, has meetings scheduled with several members of her team, and thanks to the points she has earned and redeemed, has a VIP ticket to the Black Mesa party.

The Power of 10 is present everywhere she looks—big displays with the team standings and live scrolling newsfeeds of user activity, attendees with their team names and colors prominently displayed on their badges, and QR codes on badges and at sessions so she can check in. And, of course, she's using her AC15 mobile app to do all of it.

A new set of missions has gone live as well, including a mix of universal ones (scan other people and answer their "Ask Me" questions correctly) and others targeted to her based on her registration questions. She scans people while waiting in line for lunch and to get into keynotes and has fun interacting with them around their "I Am A" descriptions and "Ask Me" questions, and those conversations starters often lead her into interesting discussions or at the least a good laugh.

There are points to be earned by checking into the sessions that you signed up for, and the presenters have all created pre-session trivia games (like when you go to the movies) that you can earn points by playing, which actually makes it fun to get there early. They're also asking questions during the sessions, and if you answer them correctly, they hand you a QR code that gives you points. When she does well, her entire team benefits.

This drives her to participate, especially because her team has entered ApCon still in fourth place. They're closing in on the million points, but she really wants to get into the top three. She sees that you can earn points for filling out postsession surveys—and you earn more the sooner you fill them out! Within an hour of the end of the session gets you 10 points, longer than an hour gets you 5 points, longer than a day gets you 1 point—so she tries to do them quickly while everything is still fresh in her head.

Anytime Laura sees one of her fellow Red Team members (which is thousands of people), they exchange a smile, and she taps her badge. She raises a fake suspicious eyebrow at members of other teams, especially the ones ahead of the Red Team. It gives her a reason and the ability to break the ice with anyone—because they're all part of the same experience.

There are also missions to visit and scan QR codes at all the Aperture booths and booths in the sponsor pavilion, replacing the paper stamp cards that she's seen at other conferences. For completing those missions, she earns T-shirts and chances to win prizes. So, in her free time between sessions, Laura makes her way around the show floor and "checks in" at all the booths. She's already read about many of the sponsors via her pre-ApCon missions, so she feels empowered as she talks to the vendors about their products.

At one point during the day, in the team forum, she reads that there's a "Flash Mob" in the lobby of Moscone North and that if 250 members of the Red Team show up and check in, they each get 50 points. She runs over and breathlessly joins the crowd, and her team gets over 300 people there and a big slug of bonus points. A big cheer goes up from the crowd of red badges. Crazy!

When her team hits the million Aperture Point milestone, Gordon Freeman sends out a congratulatory message and encourages them to earn as many points as they can during the remaining days of ApCon. She's relieved that they completed their main mission, but now her competitive drive kicks in, and she wants to be #1, so she's fully engaged and participating as much as she can—and enjoying every minute of it.

At the closing keynote, Aperture CEO Cave Johnson makes a point of talking about the Power of 10 and the Aperture Foundation. He talks about how ApCon started 10 years ago and how it's grown at an exponential rate. Then he shows the current team standings and announces the final standings. The Red Team comes in second! Not as good as first, but Laura will take it— second place earns an extra $10,000 for the foundation!

Cave talks about how the ApCon community has worked together to provide thousands of dollars to fund meaningful charity efforts. He shares what some of the raised money is going to go toward. Then the members of his exec team who were team leaders join him on stage and talk about the extraordinary efforts that their teams made, and they talk about some of the people they met in the process. It's an inspirational session, and Laura leaves energized and inspired. She never expected this when she signed up for ApCon, but it was an experience that she'll never forget, and she can't wait to see what they do next year because she'll be back.

After ApCon

Coming back from ApCon and back into the real world was honestly a bit of a letdown. It had been such an incredible experience for Laura that she hadn't wanted it to end. When she got home, however, she found that there was a final mission to complete—it was to take a survey about her ApCon experience. And if 90 percent or more of her team completed it within a week, then they'd unlock another $5,000 bonus grant for the Aperture Foundation.

She filled out the survey and then posted to her team forum encouraging everyone else to do so as well. She also went to her new "People I Met" tab in the Power of 10 app and sent direct messages to all the people she met. It was a good excuse to reach out to them anyway—she'd met several people who could be useful if she ever needed technical help or even in the event that she was looking to change jobs.

She also noticed that two new badges had been added to her profile—one was "Changed the World at ApCon 2015," and the other was "Second Place in the Power of 10 at ApCon 2015." There was a message with them saying that these were now a permanent part of her profile and would show to others her experience and part in the ApCon 2015 conference for years to come. That felt nice, being acknowledged for her participation and knowing that the "badge of honor" would make her stand out next year.

Laura ends her ApCon 2015 The Power of 10 experience feeling like a contributing, active member of the Aperture ecosystem and community, that Aperture is a company like no other, and that through her affiliation with Aperture, she can make a meaningful difference in the world.

Key Design Drivers for the Power of 10

The key design drivers for the Power of 10 are that it's personal, it's collaborative, and it's rewarding.

It's Personal

ApCon attendees span a wide range of experience, Aperture products, and job roles. A one-size-fits-all approach will feel shallow and will risk confusing and alienating participants. This is how we make it personal:

- New ApCon users will get a "Welcome to ApCon" mission

that teaches them about ApCon and onboards them. Moderate users will get missions that showcase more advanced tips and techniques, and veterans will be given missions to help newer people.

- Developers will have missions related to coding, whereas trainers will have missions related to education. Each role will be assigned missions relating specifically to that role.

- Users of Portal 2.0 will be given missions that assume knowledge of Portal 2.0. Attendees who do not use Portal 2.0 will be given missions that teach them about the Portal 2.0 functionality and also can drive them to the physical booth at ApCon. The same will apply to all other Aperture products.

- Using this system, all attendees will have a mix of universally shared missions and ones that are tailored specifically to their job role, product knowledge, and ApCon experience.

It's Collaborative

ApCon is *huge*. An experience focused solely on individuals won't work. With so many people there, it becomes hard to connect in any meaningful way with other people and is easy to just be a faceless part of the crowd. This is how ApCon makes it collaborative:

- The key to dealing with a huge number of participants is teams. Every attendee is assigned to one of 10 teams, and team members are readily identified by a color and team name on their badge. Teams work together to earn points (leveraging individuals' unique knowledge and skill sets — see "It's Personal") and compete with other teams to raise money for the Aperture Foundation. This setup creates a social unit for attendees to identify and bond with, creates friendly competition, and unifies the entire community toward a common charitable goal.

- Individuals still can be showcased and rewarded, but the key unit is the team.

- Leaderboards now become meaningful to everyone because all the teams are on them. If you had an individual leaderboard, it would only engage the top 100 participants.

- All participants can make a contribution to their team, no matter how small.

It's Rewarding

Prosocial incentives (rewards that you give to other people rather than keep for yourself) have been shown to increase employee performance more than standard incentives do. The key is to use a mix of both. This is how we make it rewarding:

- The team goal is primarily a prosocial one, with everyone working together to raise money for the Aperture Foundation.

- Individuals can earn points through stellar performance on their missions and then redeem them for rewards in a reward store. These rewards should not be cash and dollar-value prizes, aside from possibly standard corporate gear such as T-shirts. They should primarily be about enhancing the attendee's ApCon live experience. Being showcased on the big screens, guaranteed or early access to keynotes, special seating at the concert, exclusive parties or meet and greets with Aperture executives, and so on. Things that are low or no cost to Aperture but meaningful to attendees.

Notes

Chapter 1

1. www.colloquy.com/files/2011-COLLOQUY-Census-Talk-White
   -Paper.pdf.

2. http://chiefmarketer.com/incentives/customer_loyalty_barry_kirk
   _promo_1004_peo9.

3. www.adobe.com/engagement/pdfs/Forrester_TLP_How_Engaged
   _Are_Your_Customers.pdf.

4. www.jfklibrary.org/Research/Ready-Reference/RFK-Speeches/Day
   -of-Affirmation-Address-news-release-text-version.aspx.

5. www.gallup.com/strategicconsulting/157451/state-american-work
   place-2008-2010.aspx.

6. www.fi.nielsen.com/site/documents/NielsenTrustinAdvertising
   GlobalReportApril2012.pdf.

7. http://business.time.com/2012/03/29/millennials-vs-baby-boomers
   -who-would-you-rather-hire/.

8. http://edition.cnn.com/2012/08/20/business/generation-y-global
   -office-culture/index.html.

9. http://business.time.com/2012/03/29/millennials-vs-baby-boomers
   -who-would-you-rather-hire/.

10. http://blogs.hbr.org/cs/2011/12/millennials_are_playing_with_y.
    html.

11. http://blog.viacom.com/2012/10/consumer-insights-mtvs-no-collar
    -workers/.

12. http://business.time.com/2011/10/18/how-to-work-at-home-4-ways
    -to-convince-your-boss/.

13. http://online.wsj.com/article/SB1000142405311190348090457651
    2250915629460.html.

Chapter 2

1. http://www.businessdictionary.com/definition/motivation.html.

2. Daniel Pink, *Drive: The Surprising Truth About What Motivates Us*, New York: Riverhead Books/Penguin, 2010.

3. www.selfdeterminationtheory.org/theory.

4. http://en.wikipedia.org/wiki/ROWE.

5. http://www.gore.com/en_xx/aboutus/culture/index.html.

6. http://www.valvesoftware.com/company/Valve_Handbook_LowRes.pdf.

7. www.youtube.com/watch?v=soYKFWqVVzg (at 11:33 in the video).

8. http://mindsetonline.com/whatisit/about/index.html.

9. www.macworld.com/article/1162827/steve_jobs_making_a_dent_
   in_the_universe.html.

10. Teresa Amabile and Steven Kramer, *The Progress Principle: Using
    Small Wins to Ignite Joy, Engagement, and Creativity at Work,*
    Boston: Harvard Business Review Press, 2011.

Chapter 3

1. http://hbr.org/2012/10/big-data-the-management-revolution/ar/pr.

2. www.gartner.com/it-glossary/big-data/.

3. www.economist.com/node/15557443.

4. http://knowwpcarey.com/article.cfm?cid=25&aid=1171.

5. http://hbr.org/2012/10/big-data-the-management-revolution/ar/pr.

6. http://knowwpcarey.com/article.cfm?cid=25&aid=1171

7. www.mckinsey.com/~/media/McKinsey/dotcom/Insights%20
   and%20pubs/MGI/Research/Technology%20and%20Innovation/
   Big%20Data/MGI_big_data_exec_summary.ashx.

8. www.huffingtonpost.com/2010/08/05/google-ceo-eric-schmidt-
   p_n_671513.html.

9. http://online.wsj.com/article/SB100008723963904438903045780 0
   6252019616768.html.

10. http://online.wsj.com/article/SB100008723963904438903045780 0
    6252019616768.html.

11. http://smallbusiness.foxbusiness.com/legal-hr/2012/06/12/despite
    -unemployment-numbers-companies-cant-find-workers/.

12. www.reuters.com/article/2009/04/15/us-usa-workplace-reviews-
    idUSTRE53D6WV20090415.

13. http://psycnet.apa.org/index.cfm?fa=buy.
    optionToBuy&id=1996-02773-003.

Chapter 4

1. http://en.wikipedia.org/wiki/Magic_Circle_(virtual_worlds).

2. http://en.wikipedia.org/wiki/Self-determination_theory.

3. www.wired.co.uk/magazine/archive/2011/08/ideas-bank/dan-ariely.

Chapter 5

1. *Sources:* Interview with Jesse Redniss on 11/16/2012; *Forrester Report,* "Case Study: USA Network Wins Over Fans Through Gamification," by Elizabeth Shaw, 9/28/2011; www.forrester.com/Case+Study+USA+Network+Wins+Over+Fans+Through+Gamification/fulltext/-/E-RES60285?objectid=RES60285; MIT Technology Review article comments by Jesse Redniss: www.technologyreview.com/news/426127/startups-like-bunchball-turn-brands-into-games/#comments; www.emmys.com/shows/psych-hashtag-killer.

2. Interview with Jesse Redniss on 11/16/2012.

3. www.technologyreview.com/news/426127/startups-like-bunchball-turn-brands-into-games/.

4. www.forrester.com/Case+Study+USA+Network+Wins+Over+Fans+Through+Gamification/fulltext/-/E-RES60285?objectid=RES60285.

5. www.forrester.com/Case+Study+USA+Network+Wins+Over+Fans+Through+Gamification/fulltext/-/E-RES60285?objectid=RES60285.

6. www.forrester.com/Case+Study+USA+Network+Wins+Over+Fans+Through+Gamification/fulltext/-/E-RES60285?objectid=RES60285.

7. www.technologyreview.com/news/426127/startups-like-bunchball-turn-brands-into-games/#comments.

8. www.emmys.com/shows/psych-hashtag-killer.

9. Interview with Jesse Redniss on 11/16/2012.

10. *Sources:* Looking at the site; http://es.mtvema.com/press/press-2012-immersive-media; www.guardian.co.uk/technology/apps-blog/2011/nov/17/mtv-ema-apps-strategy.

11. http://es.mtvema.com/press/press-2012-immersive-media.

12. www.guardian.co.uk/technology/appsblog/2011/nov/17/mtv-ema-apps-strategy.

13. *Sources:* www.empowermm.com/blog/2011/05/18/chiquita-rio-empower-gamification/; www.1to1media.com/view.aspx?DocID=32943&PreviewMode=full&alias=bestpractice; http://chiefmarketer.com/gaming/rio_universal-studios-gamification0412peo2.

14. www.empowermm.com/blog/2011/05/18/chiquita-rio-empower-gamification/ (1:38 in the video).

15. www.prnewswire.com/news-releases/universal-studios-home-entertainment-launches-minion-madness-to-roll-out-blu-ray-and-dvd

-release-of-despicable-me-106954198.html.

16. www.resource.com/project/hp-case-study/.

17. http://hyfn.com/work/wendys-fryforall/.

18. www.a4r4.com/rightguard.

19. *Source:* insiderrewards.warnerbros.com/.

20. *Sources:* www.slideshare.net/markyolton/sap-digital-social-commu nities-briefing-book; http://scn.sap.com/docs/DOC-18427.

21. Quote from http://sloanreview.mit.edu/feature/sap-using-social -media-for-building-selling-and-supporting/.

22. *Sources:* http://topliners.eloqua.com/community/see_it/ blog/2012/10/05/eloquas-chart-of-the-week-are-community-mem bers-motivated-by-gamification; Looking at site.

23. http://marketwatch.com/story/eloqua-sees-customer-engagement -soar-SS-percent-after-deploying-bunchball-powered-jive -gamification-module-2013-03-20.

24. http://www.computerworld.com/s/article/9223627/Gamification_ goes_mainstream.

25. http://www.redding.com/news/2011/aug/14/civilization-comes-to -reddingcom/

26. http://www.computerworld.com/s/article/9223627/Gamification_ goes_mainstream

27. *Sources:* Interview with Michael Torok from SolarWinds.

Chapter 6

1. *Sources:* Interview with Richard Tate, Nicole Guthrie, and Lance Henderson from HopeLab/Zamzee; http://blog.zamzee. com/2012/10/17/whats-the-difference-between-a-pedometer-an -accelerometer-and-zamzee/; http://blog.zamzee.com/2012/08/31/ how-to-motivate-kids-to-start-exercising-and-stick-with-it/; www. hopelab.org/innovative-solutions/zamzee/zamzee-research -results/; www.zamzee.com/for_parents; http://blog.zamzee. com/2012/09/05/a-million-minutes-of-activity-the-greenfield -hebrew-academy-middle-school-gets-moving-with-zamzee/.

2. Discussion with Richard Tate, 11/1/2012.

3. http://proteus.digital.health.com.

4. *Sources:* Mira Dontcheva and Petar Karafezov, "Using Game Me- chanics to Teach Complex Software," submitted for CHI2013 (the 2013 ACM SIGCHI Conference on Human Factors in Comput- ing Systems; see the website http://chi2013.acm.org/); interviews

with Petar Karafezov and Mira Dontcheva; comments by Tacy Trowbridge on a gamification panel.

5. *Source:* http://ribbonhero.com/news.html.

6. *Source:* "The Gamification of p2p: Ford of Canada's National Dealer Training Program," provided by Maritz Canada.

7. *Sources:* www.khanacademy.org/about.

8. *Sources: The Multiplayer Classroom,* www.amazon.com/Multiplayer -Classroom-Designing-Coursework-Game/dp/1435458443.

9. http://duolingo.com/#/info.

10. Content sourced from www.rit.edu/news/magazine_story. php?id=49004.

11. Direct quote from www.rit.edu/news/magazine_story.php?id=49004.

Chapter 7

1. hbr.org/2008/07/putting-the-service-profit-chain-to-work/ar/1.

2. *Sources:* www.managementexchange.com/story/distributed-social -workforce-drives-profit-and-performance; www.liveops.com; and www.hreonline.com/HRE/print.jhtml?id=533342586.

3. www.hreonline.com/HRE/print.jhtml?id=533342586.

4. http://www.managementexchange.com/story/distributed-social -workforce-drives-profit-and-performance.

5. http://www.bunchball.com/blog/post/825/guest-post-preventing -death-powerpoint

6. *Sources:* www.btobonline.com/article/20120611/ WEB05/306119997/bluewolf-uses-employee-gamification-to -increase-social-sharing; www.dmnews.com/inbound-marketing -success-is-childs-play-for-bluewolf/article/267774/; www.marketing sherpa.com/article/case-study/gamification-effort-increases-web -traffic#.

7. www.merriam-webster.com/dictionary/reputation.

8. *Source:* Cheri Speier and Viswanath Venkatesh, "The Hidden Minefields in the Adoption of Sales Force Automation Technologies," *Journal of Marketing* 66/3 (July 2002), pp. 98–111, available at http://www.jstor.org/stable/3203457?origin=JSTOR-pdf.

9. www.zdnet.com/blog/projectfailures/crm-failurerates-2001 -2009/4967.

10. http://blogs.aberdeen,com/customer-management/sales-effective ness-2013-the-riseof-gamification.

Chapter 8

1. www.huffingtonpost.com/scott-barry-kaufman/does-creativity
   -require-c_b_948460.html.

Chapter 9

1. http://en.wikipedia.org/wiki/Interaction_design.
2. http://steveblank.com/2009/10/08/get-out-of-my-building/.
3. http://blog.intuit.com/trends/what-is-a-follow-me-home/.
4. www.managementexchange.com/story/distributed-social-workforce
   -drives-profit-and-performance.
5. www.nngroup.com/articles/why-you-only-need-to-test-with-5-users/.
6. http://en.wikipedia.org/wiki/Perfect_is_the_enemy_of_good.
7. http://en.wikipedia.org/wiki/Website_wireframe.

Index

About the Author

Widely recognized as the father of gamification, **Rajat Paharia** founded Bunchball in 2005. Since then, he has parlayed his unique understanding of technology and design—along with a preternatural ability to recognize patterns— into the creation of a company whose market-defining solutions have helped engage customers and motivate employees at a wide array of companies, including Toyota, Mattel, T-Mobile, Bravo, VMware, ESPN, BOX Technologies, and Kimberly Clark. Before founding Bunchball, Rajat had built a technology design career at IDEO, Philips Consumer Electronics, IBM Research, and ViewStar. A graduate of Stanford University and the University of California, Berkeley, he lives in Fremont, California, with his wife and three sons.